Kathleen Depperschmidt

LET'S DO 52 LUNCHES

A Year of Connecting

D1711024

TABLE OF CONTENTS

LET'S DO LUNCH

We should do lunch sometime.
(Me, or the other person I know.)

Yeah, that sounds great.
(The other one responds.)

Great! Let's get in touch soon and figure out when.
(Again, me or someone I know.)

Okay. Take care and have a great day!
(Other person responds.)

Thanks! You, too!
(Me, them.)

But we won't, because we never do, I'd say to myself as I walked away.

I'd had enough of this nonsense, so I decided to do something about it.

On December 1st, 2010, I began the first of my 52 weekly lunch dates. For the next year—plus one month—I took someone different to lunch. Someone I needed to reach out to, or someone I needed to spend more time with. I only needed one extra week to fit them all in, with the expectation that this would be wrapped up in short order, after each of those 52 dates fulfilled their end of the deal: they had to reach out to someone they needed to connect with and take them to lunch. Just one. Then they had to report back to me with their stories.

Most of them did this in short order, with no problems. Some took a little longer. Some took a long time. Some took even longer. Some required gentle prompts, then prodding from me to get it done. Some didn't do it. Some faded away, and I couldn't reach them after that. I remain a little heartbroken about those few, but I have blessed them and continue to send them good vibes.

Finding 52 lunch dates may seem like a daunting task to most people, but not to me. People tell me I have a knack for making and keeping friends, so I decided to believe them. Doesn't everyone collect friends like I do?

Apparently not.

Was I a little unrealistic, a little crazy to think I could pull this off? Apparently so.

Still, I had to do it. I promised 52 people I would, and I have to keep up my end of the deal. As the year progressed, I realized there were people I should have taken to lunch, but my list was filled up—52 people, and no more were allowed, by definition.

Then I realized I was making the rules, so I broke them, and changed them to make it work for me. I took more time, I let it slide, I rolled my eyes at myself for conceiving and trying to pull off such a crazy stunt and tried to ignore this living thing I had given birth to. It became a grand effort, and I wasn't sure I could complete it.

But I had to; I am a woman of my word. So, I did.

I wanted to fill in the gaps that were left by those dates who ultimately didn't become part of this finished product. I reached out to those people —beyond the initial 52—who needed to be included in the project. They are included in the Bonus Dates at the end.

**

Thanksgiving is my favorite holiday. There are no commercial expectations, merely an expectation to express gratitude and eat until you can't eat anymore, and then eat a little bit more. Then you do it all over again with leftovers all weekend. I love it. I don't shop on Black Friday, I'm not that kind of girl. I typically spend the weekend at the home of my oldest sister, just over three hours west and a bit north of my home. We do go out to the small hometown Main Street in her town Friday evening for an hour or so of specials, but none of the pre-dawn stuff. I don't get up at that hour unless I am catching a flight or giving birth.

So, we eat. A lot. My sister is gracious enough to allow each of us our respective in-laws' dinner on Thursday, but we are expected to be there for the weekend. Only ice, snow or vomiting will keep us away, or excuse our absence.

It's Gail's house. You *must* be there.

I was there in 2010, as usual. It was grand, as usual. We gave a lot of thanks. We all have many reasons to give thanks. Despite our shared losses, we remain grateful.

**

Sunday brings the trip home. My husband, our two sons and I eat yet another delicious turkey variation for lunch Sunday, and hit the road, just in time for the NFL feature game of the day on the radio, featuring the team three hours in the other direction from us on Interstate 70.

I couldn't possibly care any less about this barbaric face-off, so I offer up good luck to them (Go, Chiefs). In order to escape the auditory hell that football on the radio is for me in an enclosed vehicle for three hours with three guys, I plug into my music and let my mind wander to one of my many happy places, and some less-than-happy places, but they do need to be visited in order to take care of business.

One of these places presents itself to me today. Just last week, I spoke the first words at the beginning of this story, and I felt the top of my brain beg to explode out of my head.

"*I can't keep saying this and not meaning it,*" my brain screamed. "*I simply won't do it again.*"

So, in a completely novel twist, I decided to listen to the little-turned-large voice. I decided to honor the wisdom within that, too often, I shush. I calm it down with *but I'm too busy, and that's okay, because everyone else is, too.*

"Busy" is the new badge of honor. If we are not "busy," then surely, we must be lazy. And *that*, well—lazy is just not acceptable. Un-American, even. So "busy" it is. We are all "busy," so it must be okay.

It's not.

It's not okay to be too busy for your friends. It's not okay to not make time to see your friends for lunch or otherwise. We make time for our families—this should be the bare minimum, and most of us don't even do enough of that. We spend time as if it is a replaceable commodity like money, like we can make more of it.

We can't. We don't know how much time we have. We all know that, but somehow, we don't bother to apply it to our lives.

That lesson was presented to me the hard way, and my life continues to be an ongoing effort to continue to learn it. It is a journey, not a destination. Now, 15 years after that one moment, and twelve years after I started this project, I am wrapping this up. I took too much of that precious time that is not granted, but I obviously did finally complete this epic project.

In that less-than-happy-but-necessary place I visited in my mind that Thanksgiving Sunday in the car, I made a decision: I would never say "Let's do lunch" ever again if I didn't mean it.

In the next 53 weeks, starting a few days later on December 1st, I would say it 52 times, and I would mean it every time. I would reach out to 52 people I needed to connect with, or simply spend quality time with, and they would agree to one expectation in return: they would pay-it-forward by reaching out to just one person they needed to connect with, someone that they knew they needed to see again, and it had to be at least a bit of a stretch.

Just one. I, however, had to reach out to 52 people. I started to make a list, and rather than coming up short, I had to cross off a few names. These people were as close geographically as my husband, and as far away as Minnesota. They were as young as my quarter-century niece and stepson, and as old as *just a few months away from heaven,* even though we weren't sure at the time exactly when that would be. They were as familiar as kindergarten classmates, and as new to me as the new year on the calendar.

Call me crazy. Go ahead, just do it, because I am—at least a little bit. That became more apparent as I completed the dates and tried to follow up to get their pay-it-forward stories. That was the other end of the deal. They had to let me know, either verbally or in writing, how it went. I will take full blame for those shortcomings because who *really* thought I would pull this off? I don't blame them if they didn't take me seriously or, worse, if my explanation of this convoluted idea didn't make any sense to them. Whatever the reason, some people were harder to pin down than others. Some didn't respond with their pay-it-forward date, and that's okay. I have blessed them, and I give thanks for the lunch date we had. Still, I am so glad they were part of this project. They were meant to be one of the chosen 52—plus.

The *plus* is this: in place of those people who didn't follow up, or who decided they would rather not be a part of it after careful consideration, I filled in the gaps. I tried to have one date per week during that year, but you will notice some weeks are absent of any lunch dates. There were a few weeks when I couldn't schedule one, but in the end, there were several weeks when I didn't include my lunch date for that week. The "bonus" lunch dates I included after the original ones are

4

included in the end; they were added as time went along. Although no one single date could be replaced in my heart, I did substitute these bonus dates at the end in lieu of the ones I left out.

Welcome to my year of lunch dates. If you were one of those dates, I cannot thank you enough. If you were one of my date's dates, thank you for being part of this project, and thanks to all of you for your patience.

AFTER THE LAST DATE

I started this project because I wanted to share a lesson learned. That lesson, of course, was that life is short, and I learned it in just *one moment*. I thought I fully learned it—the hard way, of course. I wanted my lunch dates to learn it the easy way. I realize now it is never fully learned, and the lesson is ongoing and lifelong. The learning will always be present tense, and if I think I have fully learned the lesson, that just means I have so much more to learn.

After my year and one month of *52 Lunches,* I didn't go out to lunch very often. I didn't plan to keep up that breakneck pace; it was an intense year of lunching out for me. Nor did I plan on returning to my old patterns; I wanted to take that lesson and apply it more frequently in my life, meeting somewhere in the middle between the two extremes. Not just for lunch dates, but for maintaining contact more closely with the people I cared about. While I think I was pretty good at that before *52 Lunches*—at least people told me I was—I thought I would get even better. I thought I would make a stronger commitment to staying in closer touch with many of my dates. Somehow, I thought things would change—I thought *I* would change. Perhaps, foolishly, I thought the world around me would change.

It didn't. And *I* didn't change as much as I'd hoped I would. I wanted to give myself a new and more profound sense of time and its value. Having foolishly thought that I fully learned that lesson too— that time is fleeting and more valuable than any of us know—I feel that I did heighten this sense, but it is too easy to go back to one's old patterns, so I did. Too often, I found myself wasting precious time, time I could have used to stay connected and stay in awe of it all. Humans tend to do that, and I am human.

This painful awareness came back to bite me throughout the *52 Lunches* year (and one month). I slogged through the pain and torture and ultimate joy that is necessary to bring to life new creations with my first two books, much like gestation and childbirth. I wanted to complete them before this one, since they had been lingering for quite some time. Oh, and I did work, like, *at a paid day job*. I continued to provide speech therapy as a private contractor, and for a home health agency. Not full-time, but enough time to take up a significant amount of my day. As I rank these priorities in the form of an excuse, I must add that I did try to elevate and prioritize my roles as mother and wife above all else. My mother set a very good example of how to do just that, as I aspire to fill those roles half as well as she did.

All disclaimers aside, I did finally finish the project—obviously.

$$**$$

After the 52 lunch dates, I went back to the path of least resistance. I went back to not seeing these people again. I went back to eating my lunch in my car between appointments. I let too many opportunities to connect again slide away from me. I returned to the rut. Many of my lunch dates required multiple prompts to return their stories to me, either in written or spoken form so that I could write them, and some didn't return them at all. I will shoulder a considerable portion of the responsibility for the delayed response; perhaps my plan was not clear, even though I thought it was. Perhaps, because I had yet to produce an actual written book—a book that *I* actually wrote—they didn't believe I really would write a book about the *52 Lunch Dates*. I wouldn't blame them if they didn't believe me. I hope they believe me now, several years after I launched the project, two books in hand with my name authoring them, and a renewed commitment to get this book done.

This was really no way to write a book, but I did it this way anyway. I waxed. I waned. I slacked. I wrote. I didn't write. I was in denial. I denied that I was in denial. Then I moved on. I actually finished the book.

The toughest realization is this: Nothing changed. I don't know if I expected my life to take some cosmic and life-altering turn by completing the 52 dates. Perhaps I thought I would stay in closer touch with these people after the year was up. Maybe I thought I would develop some superhuman ability to maintain these 52 relationships on a much grander scale than I was already.

I really didn't, and here's the kicker: I am okay with that.

I have read in more than one article that, as we age, we tend to pare down the number of true friends and focus on those with whom we feel the strongest connections and continue to forge them. I can see that I am definitely a human in that respect. I love each and every one of those 52-plus people, and some are a permanent fixture in my life as family members, but most of them will remain *just friends*. Not super-human friends, not closer friends, just friends. Just like they were before this project started.

**

That *one moment* I spoke of must be explained. I wanted to breeze over it, or perhaps leave it out altogether, but it is the inspiration for this book. It is heavy stuff, but it is the stuff of life—and death, and it cannot be left out.

My six siblings—two sisters, four brothers—and I were blessed with incredible parents. On March 4th, 2008, they were killed in a car accident. They were driving home the day after our grandmother's funeral.

Their lives were a testament to their love for us. Our lives, from that point on, have been lived in an effort to live out that legacy. This project is one way I am attempting to do just that.

**

There is a friend who helped me get this project done, because it was bigger than me getting it done on my own. After much, much too long, I had help. Her name was Gina. Gina wasn't one of the 52 lunch dates, but, in essence, she was all of them. She is now one of all of us, and she gave me the strength I needed to make it all the way. I learned a lot from her. I'll call that wisdom "The Lesson."

GINA'S LESSON: THE LUNCH DATE I DIDN'T HAVE

October 13th, 2013: I visited Gina today at the hospice. She moved here three days ago. I didn't take her to lunch as part of this project. I regret that.

Gina is 39 years old. She has a glioblastoma: an incurable brain cancer—the same kind that took her mother. Gina is an occupational therapist; I met her as a third of the local therapy trifecta: physical, occupational and speech therapy. In our small city, in these professional specialties, most of us know each other.

We were not close friends, nor were we old friends. We became acquainted professionally and bonded personally. We both lost our parents too soon, too young. Her father passed away several years before her mother. Her 29-year-old brother passed away suddenly several years before that. She has one remaining brother, and she is single with no children. Our losses were our common bond.

After I completed the last of my 52 dates, I heard the heartbreaking news about Gina from a physical therapist. Too much time had passed since our last visit, and I needed to connect with her again. I had to tell her I didn't invite her to lunch as part of the project. I knew she would understand.

She did. A year after the other dates were done, we went to lunch. I told her I wished I had included her, but I had a better idea: I would dedicate this book to her. She smiled inside and out, and said, "That would be so cool."

Today, as I sat visiting with Gina at the hospice, I read the first part of the book to her. She can no longer see well enough to read. Once again, she smiled from the heart, and said, "I love it."

This opened a door for a heart-to-heart talk I will never forget. She wanted to express her love for me and everyone else, and this is what she said. I quickly scribbled down her words because I knew they were gold, and I didn't want to let a single one get away:

"I wish I could do it better. I know it's different; I can't write it down or say it like I want, but I'm going to do it with music, hugs or smiles because that's what I still have to do." I corrected her to the present tense, informing her that "You ARE doing it." She continued:

"If at some point it doesn't come out how I want it to, it's just being here. Even if it's just sitting beside each other with a touch."

These words from Gina are more precious to me than gold.

**

As I continue to write this chapter, Gina's health continues to decline. I visit her at the hospice about once each week, but the family and staff have asked to keep our visits brief. Gina fatigues easily, and it is difficult for her to fully engage as she would like to, but she keeps on trying—sometimes too hard. I am one of a multitude of friends who visit her, and I feel guilty because I know my visits benefit me more than they do her. She gives, and I take. I cry, and she laughs. I don't need a lot of her; a little of her love and energy stays with you long after you leave. I am at peace with her likely leaving us because she is at peace. We agreed in an earlier visit that miracles can happen, but neither of us is planning on one. We are planning accordingly. We are relishing each moment that is granted to us together on this earth. She knows where she is going, and who is waiting there for her. She is okay now, and she will be even more okay then. *Peace* is the key word here. But *love* is another key word.

All you need is love. Love's the only rule. When you love someone…The power of love. Music knows it's about love, and the lyrics of Gina's beloved music speaks that loud and clear for her now. When I leave after our visits, she says, "*Love…love…love.*" She suggests it gently, but I know she knows its power better than any of us. She blows kisses as I leave. *Love is all that matters. Love is all you need.* At this point in her short life, that truly is all that matters to her.

It should be all that matters to all of us as well, but we all know it is not. We are *busy* with jobs, families and obligations. Most of our families give us more love than anyone else, but I am as guilty as the next girl of giving away time and energy to things that don't love us back. Time and energy that should have been given to our families and other loved ones.

Busy. Ugh. The dreaded four-letter "b" word. Most of us are guilty of being too busy.

Gina is not busy anymore, if she ever was guilty of it—being too busy, that is. *Busy* no longer figures into her life. She doesn't have the ability to be busy anymore, she slows down more each time I see her. Busy doesn't matter to her anymore. Only love matters.

**

December 3rd, 2013: Gina's funeral was this morning. She passed away quietly with her family at her side on Thanksgiving eve. I came home early after the service today and *busied* (ugh, that word) myself around the house, getting little things done I had neglected. I hit the wall with a task that was completely confounded by forces out of my control, and I lost it. This morning I was deep inside myself, feeling the most intense emotions a human can feel—sadness and grief, faith, and hope—and now I have boxed myself back into what means nothing.

I will maintain that the greatest moral compass is in the answer to this classic question: "What would Jesus do?" However, Gina and I had discussed that since our parents died, we feel a special connection through the heart with them now, and we have a heavenly hotline of sorts when we need their advice.

"What would Mom and Dad do?" We could ask this and expect clear, personalized guidance from Above, albeit with an idea more than direct words. Now, I have another guide from Above: "What would Gina do?" I asked myself this question this afternoon. She wouldn't get upset about this inconsequential "stuff." She would laugh and move on. She would realize it was no big deal. I thought I had learned this important lesson, but clearly, I hadn't. Now, just hours after memorializing her, I am sweating the small, stupid, trivial stuff. Gina would not waste one moment of her precious time on something so meaningless, before or after her diagnosis.

So, this lesson, *The Lesson*, will not be forgotten. In her honor, I must make it a priority to do what Gina would do: She wouldn't waste one second of her precious time on something so meaningless, so inconsequential. She would let it go and focus on only that which brought her happiness. Everything else would fade away.

That is what I will try my best to do.

Because this project is dedicated to her, I will begin now with this mindset about this book: I will begin to implement The Lesson from Gina. It will be an ongoing lesson, one that will continue for weeks, months and hopefully years to come. I will not waste any more time fretting about this book, and my multiple stops and starts. It will be completed in good time, with Gina's guidance from Above. I will offer my subjects a course in The Lesson taught by Gina if they are interested. She will continue to offer lessons in The Lesson if we only let her.

The course will be ongoing, and can last for one's lifetime, if we allow it to. It is free, and it will not be graded. Perhaps we can assign ourselves our own grade. We can take the course over and over again and apply it to new situations in our lives.

Only love matters.

Please don't ever forget this lesson, *The Lesson*. More importantly, please live your life as a reflection of *The Lesson*.

**

In honor and memory of Gina Jennings: 1974-2013

FULL CIRCLE

Last night, December 21st, 2016, I observed the winter solstice, the shortest day of daylight in this year's trip around the sun. The most extreme tilt away from the source of heat and light for every living thing on our half of the planet.

Let there be light. Today, there will be more daylight. Just a few minutes more, but more, nonetheless.

I am acutely attuned to this annual cycle. Every June 21st, I relish the daylight in this, the longest day of the year that will now begin waning, a few minutes every day, but less, nonetheless. Then, I begin to fight off a funk that tries to come over me, this sure knowledge that the amount of sunlight in our days will now become shorter until this date, December 21st.

I live by the sun. I worship the sun. I need the light and the heat.

**

I had a chance encounter with my high school math teacher yesterday. We can easily fall into conversation about things more important than math. Life and love, life and loss. I didn't know this about her, but she, too, relishes the sunlight that now begins to increase daily. She, too, observes this day as the day it starts a slow turnaround. She, too, lives by the light and observes June 21st as well. I should have guessed.

We talk about the upcoming holiday and the yearning we will always feel for our loved ones we have lost, especially around this time of year. She lost her husband a few years ago, so she knows. More powerful than that, though, we talk about the sure knowledge that they are still with us, all around us; within us. *"Deep in our hearts,"* I say to her, with my hand on my heart.

Full circle. Complete. Whole. Finished. None of these words express what I want to say about today's lunch date. Perhaps I should say I closed the gap. I took a trip around the sun—six trips, actually. I had only intended to take one to finish this project. Today, six revolutions plus twenty more days—plus two leap year days added—I had my last lunch date. Two thousand, two hundred and fourteen days later. That is, if I got my math right.

I never liked math, but my teacher made it as light and fun as it could possibly be and made us realize that math is a part of life, even for those in the class like me who didn't enjoy it and had no plans to use it professionally. I think of her every time I set up an equation to convert the amounts in a recipe. That's about the only time I use algebra. But I think about her more often than that. I realize today that she could have easily been a lunch date; she is that special. The list could have gone on and on, I realize. That stretch I thought I would have to do to find 52 lunches became a stretch to limit it to only 52.

Today, I finished the loop. I stopped where it all started. I made a complete revolution. The idea was planted with a single comment from my friend Tina, whom you will meet early in the book. I ended it with a lunch date with Tina, who was a science teacher. A real lunch this time, because, as you will read, hers wasn't a real date—just coffee (December 17th). It was a date with a former science teacher. A teacher who knows—scientifically—about revolutions around the sun, and personal revolutions, as she watches her three boys go through every year as fast as mine seem to.

She observed her 45th birthday five days ago. I wanted to shoot for that day just as I had last time, but my schedule would not allow. Plus, she likely had a better deal waiting for her on her special day.

So, I settled for this day, and it was perfect. We met—her choice—at Martinelli's, our local downtown Italian gem. The hour-plus went by too quickly, but it was worth more than an hour—it was the other bookend.

Tina's teaching experience brought her to her current position, which, she tells me, requires her to wear many hats. By definition, she is an after-school program coordinator for a local teen organization. By her nature and insight, however, it doesn't start and stop in the after-school hours. She has become an angel—my word, not hers—to these families when they have needs that seem to persist but lessen thanks to people like her. She loves it, and they love her.

Her oldest son of three is at the same university as my son, and we compare tales of motherly woe and wonder at their growth, maturity, departure and sleep cycles. We are in the Boys Club, and we wouldn't trade it for anything.

**

"We should do lunch sometime."

Tina uttered those words that launched this undertaking over six years ago. The words that resonated and reverberated through my head, the words that resisted the pitfall of responding, *"But I'm too busy."*

Thank you, Tina. May you continue to show me, those lucky teenagers you mother and work with, and all the world how to pay it forward.

12/1: JANE

Today is the first of my 52 lunches. My guest of honor is Jane. It has been over one year since I told her I would take her out to lunch; I am starting with the most overdue. The kicker for Jane, though, is that I am repaying a debt by taking her to lunch. Now I am asking her for something else.

Jane is a 62-year-old retired speech therapist. When she hung it up a year ago, she generously gave me her therapy materials. She wouldn't accept payment for them, she said I could simply take her to lunch. I am so tardy with this one.

Jane and I go way back, but my husband's family goes back even further with her. My father-in-law worked for her father's company at one point. More connected than that is the fact that Jane is responsible in large part for my brother-in-law Brad's success as a profoundly hearing-impaired person in a hearing world. Brad is my husband's brother, and Jane was his first speech therapist. I wasn't in the picture then; I came on the scene only seventeen years ago. Brad was two when she started to work with him. He is 40 years old now.

Jane has lived in my small city for many years, having served as the lone speech therapist at our hospital. Prior to embarking on my graduate degree, Jane graciously allowed me to observe her in action. I loved what I saw. I proceeded with my plans to return to college to obtain a master's degree in speech-language pathology.

My dream at the time was to be the illustrious and superhuman school speech therapist. I tried that gig for four years, but the truth cannot be denied: I belonged with adults. I eventually found myself working in the very position she occupied when I observed and later interned with her as a student.

We dined today at her favorite Mexican restaurant; most any Mexican restaurant is my favorite. The food was good, but the company and conversation were even better.

I learned so much from Jane in the professional sense, and along the way she imparted her wisdom from having lived a few more years than me. Today, she freely dispensed more wisdom. She reflected on her life as a new retiree, thinking back to the major decisions she made throughout her life.

She contrasted the "*I wish*" sentiments against the "*What if?*" ideas. The "*I wishes*," she explains, are regarding the things about one's life that probably could not have been changed, but still we wonder what life might have been like if…

The "*What Ifs?*" surround the lost chances, the missed opportunities. They are the stuff of regrets. The doors we close become greater in number as life goes on and, as one ages, the thought that we can change others or external events becomes pointless, and changing oneself becomes harder, too.

She spoke of her dream as a young woman to become a hairdresser, but her parents insisted that she go to college for at least four years. She never let go of that idea. Now that she is retired, perhaps, she could fulfill that dream. Her husband was agreeable, but she knew that realistically for her, it was too late.

She didn't speak to me as if it were advice, but just like so many of her lessons, I learned from simply listening closely and reading between the lines. I like to think she is telling me that I am doing the right thing by doing my own thing, both in my writing and in my private speech therapy business. I have learned so much from her, but the learning is not over. She will continue to teach me, I know, for a long time to come.

JANE'S LUNCH DATE(S)

I won't say that I entered this profession so I could help people. That sounds too hokey—even if it is true. Partially true, that is. You will have to read the introduction to my first book to see what the other, more compelling reason was.

Jane entered this profession to satisfy her parents' desire for her to have a college education—or so she says. Something tells me she knew deep down she could make a difference in people's lives, and she needed a career that would help her do just that. I will add that, if I had to name one aspect of my work that is the most rewarding, it is just that:

I get the privilege of helping people communicate again, and *that*, I have learned, does make a difference.

It is natural that Jane would reach out to connect with someone who was important to her—that is the essence of the whole project. The reason this person was important, ironically, is because Jane is important to them.

"Charlotte" was the wife of one of Jane's patients. Charlotte's husband had a stroke and was unable to communicate. He understood most of what was spoken to him but couldn't express himself. He withdrew and didn't make the effort necessary to even try to express himself—except with Jane.

When his hospital stay was over, he required continued nursing care in a facility. There was only one local nursing home Charlotte would consider sending him to, but medically, the powers that be recommended another facility with more intense care for his specific health issues. They wouldn't agree with Charlotte's choice of facilities—until Jane made it clear to those powers that he would indeed be in the best possible hands there. He was accepted and lived peacefully for two years there until his death.

Jane and Charlotte kept in touch after his death, but Jane knew too much time had passed since their last visit. She asked Charlotte to lunch, and Charlotte knew it was time, too.

Time is a gift if we use it to show our loved ones just how much we really do love them. Charlotte used her last two years with her husband to do just that, and to thank Jane, she told her this—through tears:

"I want to tell you how much I love you. If not for you, we wouldn't have had those last two years."

Jane did make a difference, both with Charlotte and her husband.

Knowing she had another woman she needed to connect with, Jane took it one step further. There was another woman who had been married to a former patient, another woman who became her friend. Jane called her.

"Elizabeth" was the mother of two sons. Her husband had a stroke in his early 50's. He was physically functional, but not able to express himself. He could, however, understand everything said to him. They traveled and enjoyed their limited time together until her husband passed away several years after his stroke.

Elizabeth needed a ride to a doctor's appointment 100 miles away, and Jane volunteered to take her. They spent the rest of the day shopping after they enjoyed lunch—Jane's second lunch date.

"If I'd had a daughter," Elizabeth said to Jane, "I'd want her to be just like you."

These powerful words—both from Charlotte and Elizabeth—prove that what Jane told me today just might be true. I met with her today many months after our first date, and we enjoyed another lunch date. I told her how I am moving toward writing goals. Her words made me stop in my mental tracks:

"We really do make a difference," Jane said.

I have always believed this about our profession. We improve or help restore a lost ability, a wondrous ability that connects us with other human beings. Today, I see where I have been, and it has been a wonderful journey. As I look ahead, I know I can make a difference with the written word—as well as the spoken word. Jane doesn't disagree.

12/6: DOT

A nursing home patient once asked me if my co-worker Dot was my mother. She's not, but I'd sure take her as a substitute. Although she is a peer in the work sense, she is 22 years older than me, and at least that much wiser.

I have worked with Dot for almost four years, but I have known her for about thirteen years from a previous work setting. I see her at least several times a week, but just in passing. The nature of the beast in the nursing home therapy setting is that of a fly-by-night. We are there and gone, but we do honest work, and we *do* come back. Rarely do we get a chance to spend quality time visiting while on the clock, but as I write that last statement, I realize it makes me sound like a slacker. Our schedules and productivity guidelines dictate that we really don't have time to slack, as much as we would like to. Therefore, we are forced to schedule time outside of work to hang out. This is no easy feat, as we are all busy with families and other obligations. There's that word again—*busy*. I loathe what it does to us.

For months now, Dot and I have been trying to sneak out for a day and play legitimate hooky. After several failed attempts, we finally did it. We took a Monday off and snuck to Wichita to shop for Christmas, for ourselves, and to enjoy each other's company. I adore her, and while I can't speak for her, she likes me enough to agree to an entire day in my presence.

Because it took a concerted effort, it was long overdue, and because it was no easy feat, she became my second lunch date. Greater than those reasons, though, I took her to lunch because she is my friend and mentor, and quite simply, I like her.

I often tell my stroke patients that I understand their suffering, but I don't know how they feel. How could I? Even though I have worked with several thousand people who have had strokes, I have never had one.

Dot knows how they feel. She had a stroke about ten years ago. It only partially disabled her for a temporary period, but she knows the feeling of lost abilities. She carries this empathy with her into her therapy with her patients.

Dot became a certified occupational therapy assistant (COTA) later in life, after her three boys were grown. She is preparing to retire at the end of this year, in just a few short weeks. She will continue to work on an on-call basis, but no more than she wants to. What she *really* wants to do is spend more time with her grandchildren and her husband. She will, too. She will say no when she wants to because she will be able to. She will no longer be obligated to work but will likely help when there is a need *only if* she isn't busy with her family.

I often tell Dot I want to be like her when I grow up. She calls a spade a spade, and lets stress roll off her back. She laughs a lot, and makes others laugh too. We have a mutual admiration for each other's wardrobes and jewelry, even though we know we are both excessive in those respects.

So, what are we doing today? Shopping. Yes, we are shopping for other's Christmas gifts, but we do sneak in a little treat for ourselves too. We acknowledge that we can, whereas there was a time in our younger lives when we couldn't. We are aware of our excesses, so I guess that's a step in the right direction.

We make it back home by five and slide back into our domestic roles. Life is good, we agree. Life can be really good when you spend time with people you really like. I really like Dot, and I think she likes me too, even though she has to work harder than I do to fulfill all the roles I have assigned to her. Since I can no longer shop and have lunch with my mother, then Dot is a worthy substitute. Today, she fills those shoes very well.

When I got the news about our parents, and I knew I had to let my workplace know what had happened, instinctively, I knew I could call Dot, and let her take it from there. And she did. I will be forever grateful to her for bearing that weight for me.

DOT'S LUNCH DATE

Dot lives in a small town about 15 minutes north of me. She has lived there since her children were born. She has a friend, Lois, who also lived there when their children were young. Both Dot's and Lois's husbands were teachers, and they were both stay-at-home mothers.

Lois moved away in the late 1970's and eventually settled about 45 minutes away from Dot. They got in touch about once a year, then it became once every two years. Dot made a special visit when Lois's mother died, and Lois did the same when Dot's father-in-law died.

Both Dot and Lois were always willing to get together for no special reason, but it seemed the time just slipped away. Even though it did indeed slip away, it was the proverbial "as if no time had passed" every time they got together. In Dot's words, being in the company of Lois was as comfortable "as an old pair of shoes."

Last year, Dot made a trip to Abilene to shop. She hadn't contacted Lois, but knew she needed—and wanted—to visit Lois. Instead of shopping, Dot stopped in to see Lois unannounced, and spent her afternoon visiting Lois instead of shopping.

Lois became Dot's choice when it came time to pick her lunch date. They spent two hours dining at Martinelli's in Salina, then shopped downtown afterwards. Their usual topics—kids, life—were discussed, just as they always are. That was their pattern all these years, and it needed to be kept up. Lois argued when Dot paid but understood that she needed to pay it forward instead. I don't know Lois, but if Dot has kept her around this long, I know she is the kind of woman who will reach out and do just that.

12/17: TINA

Tina told me she forgot that it was her birthday when I asked her out to eat on the 17th. I'm not buying it. She didn't even eat anything with me; she'd just had lunch with her kids at school for a special mother/child luncheon. She *did* have a cup of coffee. I had to keep her as my lunch date; it was Friday of the third week of my project, and it was too late to try to find another. More than that, though, she was worth it, and her kids needed her for lunch more than I did. She and I don't get together enough, and I am taking her word without a doubt that she will indeed find a pay it forward lunch date of her own.

On this date, Tina turns 39 years old—really. I know she's not lying about her age. I've known her too long. Which is precisely why, when just three and one-half weeks ago we said we should have lunch, I knew this time we simply *must*.

When she first suggested a lunch date, I smiled and nodded in agreement that it would indeed be a good idea, but inside I'm hearing myself say, *"but we won't."* We won't, because I say this quite often, and I don't make an effort to see it through. As I mentioned in the introduction, I decided I was through with these empty and meaningless agreements. It was time to change that. I give her a huge amount of credit for the motivation behind this book. That was *her* I referred to.

I met Tina sixteen years ago when I worked as a school-based speech therapist. Tina was a teacher in one of the four schools I covered. I was drawn to her smile, her infectious laughter, and her good nature. Our bond strengthened when we both joined "The Boys Club": both of us became the mother of sons. She has three, I have two of my own, and a bonus stepson. I joined the club only one year before her, she followed suit and didn't stop until three.

As usual, we laughed a lot when we got together. If she were to tell you about our friendship and the funniest moments, she would likely share this next one with you. It was funny then, it is funny now, and as long as her youngest son has any form of a speech problem, it will remain darkly funny.

I left the school-based job, and I was working at the hospital in our small city when she delivered her third child. I had the pleasure of sharing the elevator with her as she left with her new baby; she was exhausted, and I was in a hurry.

"What did you have?" I asked, excited about her third bundle of joy. I hadn't yet heard the news.

"Another boy," she replied.

"What did you name him?" I asked.

"Colby," she said. I pondered her response for only a moment, before it became obvious to me, the speech therapist:

"You'd better hope he doesn't have problems with the 'L' sound, because his name is 'Colby Bulleigh'," I said with a laugh. She laughed, too. The elevator door opened, I wished her well and we parted ways.

She will, to this day, accuse me of jinxing her son because, as you might expect, he *did* have problems with the 'L' sound. Only a speech therapist would make a comment like *this* at a moment like *that*. When he pronounced his name, it came out "Coby Bowie."

Those days are behind him now, but I will carry the blame for his early speech difficulties.

If I could use only one word to characterize our interactions, it would be *funny*. I find myself laughing more than usual when I am with her. She brings out the humor in most situations, and if a person can laugh and cry at the same time—happy or sad tears—it would be her. She can be heavy and light at the same time, she could probably even pray and cuss at the same time—although she says she prays more than she cusses. I believe her.

Tina and I share the love of running. Again, I bow down to her in her quest to run a half marathon in April, a life goal for her. I will offer the lame excuse that the few years I have on her are enough to keep me from undertaking such an endeavor, but she has given birth three times, and I have only done it twice, so I guess that excuse won't work with her. Again, I bow down to her.

We spoke of the joys of being the only female in the house. She says she doesn't have big birthday plans, nor does she expect any big surprises. The fact that she is surrounded by males keeps her expectations for birthdays relatively low, she tells me with a laugh. I get this, but I know that just like my boys—the big one and the little ones—

they love her dearly and would go to the ends of the earth and back for her.

Those boys, we agree, have taught us so much. There is no laughter when we share this sentiment. While awaiting the arrival of our second sons, we both knew there was no way we could love another baby as deeply as we loved the first one.

I don't know who shared this glowing truth with me all those years ago, but I shared it with her. No, you don't love the second—or third—any more deeply than the first, but you love them just as deep. That love, while it cannot go *deeper*, does go *wider*.

Tina and I have wide spaces in our hearts for those boys, and we know how blessed we are.

Happy Birthday, my dear friend.

TINA'S LUNCH DATE--*written by Tina*

Well, Kathleen did a great job of summarizing our relationship. Isn't it awesome how you can connect with some people? How you can be deep with them in very little time and yet laugh and not take yourself too seriously within the same moment? I will never forget how casual she was as a new mom inviting me during her lunch hour to talk to her while she pumped. I remember going from a person wondering "Where should I be looking?" to becoming a mother of three that I breastfed until they were 10 months old. Kathleen is that kind of gal. I believe God inserts people into our lives. His timing is perfect. I think God put her in my life to impart small bits of fundamental wisdom that later helped me chart my way through being a new mom. I continually feel blessed by her friendship.

Kathleen described our lunch date as a little unconventional, as we didn't really follow the rules, she set for her lunch dates. My husband teases that I tend to think that rules don't apply to me…I would like to argue with him, but I have to admit more times than not, he does speak true of my personality. So, my "pay it forward" lunch story seems to fit, as I did break the rules.

My lunch date isn't your everyday lunch date. My lunch date wasn't with someone I could physically touch or see. I don't think she ate food and I doubt that life will allow her to pay it forward any time soon. So, I did break the rules. And for the record, I did not have lunch with an imaginary friend. Instead, I had a phone lunch date with my friend in North Carolina/Nebraska, Kelli. (I will explain more soon.)

Working in a non-profit, one would liken the job to a marathon, as it is by no means a sprint. For those who run, you certainly get this analogy. A sprint is fast and tough. You go hard, but the end comes quick. This is not the case while working for a non-profit. The goals of non-profits are big and lofty. They can take days, weeks, and sometimes a lifetime to accomplish them. I often forget the marathon method of working and try to sprint. Therefore, most days I literally forget to take lunch, which is hard to imagine as I really dig food! One day in particular, I was frustrated and knew I needed to get away and take a break from it all. I hopped in my car ordered a quick meal at a nearby fast-food joint. This time, instead of rushing off as I normally do, I took the time to sit down inside, dialed my phone and took an extended hour and half lunch and enjoyed some time with my dear friend, Kelli.

Kelli is the type of person who can talk for an hour straight with nearly no pause and you aren't envious for a moment that you didn't contribute much to the conversation. She is so fascinating, as she lives life so big! Not like rock-star big, but instead, big with the biggest heart, where her heart is the leader and it takes us where, for most of us, our logic won't allow us to go because we fear the risk. She ignores all that holds the rest of us back, and she just goes for it. Her desire to go for it fascinates me.

Kelli and I were doing our master's together. I had just had a miscarriage and I knew I wanted to have my master's done before having another child. Somewhere during our 18-month stretch, Kelli's doctor told her she needed to "fish or cut bait," as she had such severe endometriosis. In essence, he was telling a single woman to get pregnant or have a hysterectomy. The weight of this was heavy on her and we talked a lot. My mind told me to weigh the options out, but her heart yearned for the child she did not yet hold. She was seeing a guy pretty steady, and he agreed to do the in vitro fertilization process. To her credit, it worked, and we both walked across the stage to receive our master's degrees, pregnant.

As life would have it, the steady guy wasn't so steady, and he left Kelli to be on her own. Being a new mother myself, I couldn't imagine going through pregnancy and delivery alone, so there was no way I would let Kelli do all this on her own, either. So, we looked like the lesbian couple who went to all the classes. I drove her to the hospital, was by her side during labor, and got to watch the c-section from the doctor's point of view. I teased her that I thought I saw her liver, so that meant we would have to be best friends forever. We chuckle over that now, but more importantly, she now held the baby girl her heart yearned for, despite the risk. She was loving big.

I felt protective of Kelli and her new little girl, but Kelli was feeling professionally unfulfilled and was wanting to seek out a new place with new opportunity. She found a job in North Carolina, which, from where I stood, was about four states too far. She didn't know a soul there, and she had this new baby girl. Who was going to help her? Her heart was telling her to go, but all I could see was the risk. She left that summer, but we talked every week. She was living big.

She ended up meeting a military guy, whom she had to question like he was a spy before she would let him into hers and her daughter's life, quizzing him about who he was and what he did for a living. His special forces status made for adventurous stories, even though she couldn't tell me the details. They married and had a daughter together. God's timing is perfect. I truly believe he was the reason she went to North Carolina. Her living big led her to loving big again.

Kelli felt their family was incomplete. They worked on fertility to the point of exhaustion, and as they started to give up, Kelli found out she was pregnant with twins. This good news was complicated with some bad news, as the pregnancy was one that could be fatal to one or both of the babies as they shared an embryonic sac. She was being encouraged to abort one of the babies. She already loved them both and could not do it. The babies were born early, but two years later they are thriving with few delays. In their naming, she used the names Hope and Faith, and I would have to say those are the two things that got her through. Loving big beat out logic again.

I felt I had to give a history of Kelli so you would know the person behind the "phone call lunch date," and so you could see why calling her would help me put my worries and frustrations into perspective. A few months before our "lunch date," Kelli had found out her mom had stage four stomach cancer. Since her husband was often absent with his military duties, she decided to pick up her four girls and rented a house in the same small town that her mom lived in, enrolling her daughters in school there. She did all this in hopes of spending another year with her mother as she fought the cancer. I knew things were not well with her mom, but I was surprised to learn that she had passed since my last phone call. It all happened so fast, within four months of her moving there. We talked about the pain of losing a parent and how to cherish your time with your loved ones. It was one of those days I did a lot of listening, as she shared with me all that she was going through. My words were few, but I felt peace knowing that she did get that time with her mom before she passed. Logic would have told a person that moving your school-aged daughters to another state is crazy, that she would have had time to come and visit later. I am so thankful she listened to her heart and not logic. She has no regrets.

Most lunch dates, you smile and laugh as you feed your physical self. You find that fancy place that has a unique menu or atmosphere. This lunch date minimally fed the physical self, but instead satisfied the emotional and spiritual self. We laughed and cried, and we had a unique menu of topics to share, while sitting in an environment that is designed to get you in and out of their establishment, and yet the friendship I was experiencing over the phone made me comfortable enough to linger longer. Yep, this lunch date wasn't like the others you may read about, but it was very filling.

12/29: SUZANNE

It is four days after Christmas…three days until the New Year. A winter storm threatens. Families continue to enjoy each other's holiday company; many people are on vacation this week. I am not, and neither is my sister, Suzanne.

I have two weeks left before my job travels will no longer take me to this town. For the last three years and nine months, I have been the speech therapist Girl Friday at the local nursing home for their infrequent speech therapy patients. My shelf life at any job appears to be between three and four years, and the jig is up—again.

Today I am dining with my little sister, Suzanne. This lunch is bittersweet; mostly sweet. We are dining on the lunch buffet at the local Pizza Hut, one of the last few times we will meet here as my work winds down. This is not just any Pizza Hut, it is the Pizza Hut our older sister Gail (July 2nd) once capably managed for seven years, until she moved several hours west. Technically, it is not the *actual* Pizza Hut she managed, because several years ago that one was razed, and this one was erected in its place.

This town is Suzanne's home now, just twenty minutes from the farm we all grew up on. I recognize many of the faces dining here today, and she knows most of them from her work at the bank. There's the nurse from the clinic; an insurance agent; a local lawyer. Oh, and that gentleman across from us, well, he was Mom and Dad's neighbor.

Aside from the welcome small towns like this naturally extend, there is a warmth here that never lets me down when I visit. *"I's born in Osborne,"* says Tracy (November 20th). I, too, was born at the small hospital here, but I never lived here. Osborne was once home to both sisters, now it is only Suzanne's home. Warmer than that, this town was my parents' home after they moved off the farm. They were driving back here when, instead, they detoured straight to Heaven. Many people here knew them, and these people still know us.

The coolest thing about my job here is that I got to see my parents about a dozen more times than I would have had I not listened to that little voice that told me to walk away from the Sure Thing where I was employed and accept this work with no guaranteed hours and an uncertain future. I stopped to visit Mom and Dad *every time* I came here—except for the one day they were off on a jaunt somewhere. Now I see Suzanne every time I can for lunch or a quick visit if there is no time for lunch; sometimes my brothers make the short trip over from the farm to join us for lunch.

While I make no bones about the fact that I yearned to push her down the stairs when she and I shared an upstairs room on the farm—she made me *that* mad when she *always* wanted to wear my clothes—we are buddies now. I wish everyone was blessed to be sandwiched between two wonderful sisters like mine. They make me laugh, and they cry with me. They mostly understand me and let me be when they don't. While I have shared the same journey through grief with all six of my siblings, it is my sisters whom I turn to the most. We keep the memories alive among all seven of us, but I have learned that women and men process grief differently. Suzanne, Gail and I understand each other.

I will tell you how I look up to my big sister Gail on July 2nd, but today I will tell you how I look up to Suzanne too, even though she is four years younger than me. Suzanne is married with a fourteen-year-old daughter, my godchild Julia. Julia is a beautiful redheaded girl; the recessive gene of the red hair remains a mystery. If you don't follow along closely, her sense of humor may be a mystery too—no recessive gene there; she gets that dry wit straight from her mother.

Suzanne was a single mother for many years, I don't know how she did it. I have a present, loving and involved father of my children, and it is still hard sometimes. She managed well and was blessed with help from Mom and Dad. There was no repayment necessary, but if there were, she likely overpaid with the time she spent with our parents.

I feel guilty for not being closer and visiting Mom and Dad more; I lived 100 miles from them and saw them every few months. She lived four blocks from them and saw them every day. She is at peace with the time spent with them. Her heart is big like that.

I was blessed to look strikingly like our mother, and Suzanne could not be easily disowned by our father. We are all blessed with their composition in body and mind, they were peacemakers *and* peacekeepers, and they left us to carry on that legacy.

I would be flattered now if she would want to wear clothes like mine. That no longer happens; perhaps she doesn't want to be like me anymore. I want to be more like her, she has talked me down from more than one ledge and commiserated when we're on the same ledge. She knows how to make me laugh when I need it and laughs *at* me when I need it. My favorite thing about her, though, is that she laughs *with* me. I'm so glad now that I didn't push her down the stairs all those years ago.

SUZANNE'S LUNCH DATE

I am so hopeful that Suzanne will soon be able to fit into my clothes, and we will once again be able to share a wardrobe. This time, it will be a wonderful thing.

Suzanne celebrated her 42nd birthday on August 16th, 2012. Except that she didn't do much celebrating. On that day, she was handed a diagnosis of thyroid cancer.

She began to lose weight early in the year. She knew something was wrong, but it took some time, persistence and sleuthing on her part to get her medical counsel to keep digging for answers. She has always had an intuitive voice that has never lied to her, and this time it kept nagging at her that *something* was indeed wrong.

There are certain words in our language that will *always* conjure negative images, never good ones. *Funeral. Debt. Hatred. Malignant. Anger. Cancer.* The "C" word, it has come to be known because it truly is unspeakable sometimes. It strikes fear into the heart of anyone who has it or loves someone who has it. It was small consolation—if any—when she was told by many medical professionals that if a person could choose their cancer, this would be the "easiest" one to have.

Jenny agreed there was nothing "easy" about thyroid cancer.

Jenny lives half an hour away from Suzanne. Suzanne found out from a flyer posted in the bank—her workplace—that there was a young woman in a neighboring town who was diagnosed with thyroid cancer, and her community was hosting a fundraiser to benefit her. She was self-employed as a hairdresser and had no health insurance. Suzanne and Jenny had a mutual friend who got them together. Suzanne was a bit further ahead in the treatment plan, so she was able to pave the way for Jenny.

After surgery to remove the entire thyroid, the treatment consisted of one dose of radioactive iodine, to be administered via capsule in a hospital, followed by two days of isolation. Exposure to others after the first two days was limited, until she was deemed to no longer be a threat. The threat to others was in the iodine, which is attracted to the thyroid like a magnet, so it would zero in on anyone else's thyroid like a target and negatively affect it. Suzanne and Jenny, as well as anyone else who receives this treatment after surgery, take the pill as a matter of course to further exterminate any trace of the diseased thyroid that may have escaped the surgeon's knife.

But this, as Suzanne and Jenny will tell you, was the easier part. Prior to taking the iodine pill, they both had to comply with a strict low-iodine diet. Due to the timing of the treatment and several factors that were out of her control, Suzanne had to be on the diet for four weeks. Jenny had to be on it for two.

If you have never had to watch your iodine intake, consider yourself lucky. Suzanne reports she became very tired of oatmeal, garbanzo beans, fruit, and vegetables. Anything with salt added had iodine, as well as many other unsuspecting edibles. It was torture.

After the treatment, she could eat whatever she wanted. Except that she didn't want many things anymore. The treatment can adversely affect taste buds, and the lack of stimulation of the taste buds prior to the treatment is a double whammy, and not much tasted good. This gradually resolved, and both Suzanne and Jenny are able to enjoy and savor their favorite foods.

So, they did—together.

Suzanne asked Jenny to be her lunch date. As was the case with many of my subjects, she didn't get it done in a timely fashion. She had all year because she was one of my first dates, and because she is my sister, I can complain about her slacking, and not getting it done.

Apparently, it was meant to be a late date. She wouldn't have met and reached out to Jenny to make a lunch date. They corresponded by email and Facebook prior to Jenny's treatment; Suzanne was able to hold her hand—figuratively speaking—and help her through the treatment. Jenny had two surgeries instead of just one, because there were unforeseen complications with her first surgery, so she was subjected to yet another surgery two weeks after her first.

Jenny is single with no children but has a close family in her small town. It *is* a small town, so when Suzanne and Jenny met for lunch at the Second Cup Café and talked for three hours, people noticed—and started talking amongst themselves.

I don't know Jenny, but I am guessing she didn't care that she was the subject of discussion as she interacted at length with this stranger. If she is anything like Suzanne—and something tells me she is—she lets it roll off her back. Tragedy has a way of doing that, of helping you put things in perspective. It may have annoyed either one of them to be made the focus of unwanted small-town attention before their lives were turned upside-down by cancer. It may have annoyed Suzanne before our parents died, but certainly not anymore. Now Suzanne and Jenny have each other as a reference point, a North Star to continue to guide each other along the road away from this "easy" cancer.

Suzanne and I—as well as our other siblings—have reflected on how our loss has made the old annoyances that used to bring us down simply minor irritations. Everything else pales in comparison.

This, my friend, is the gift of hardship. Small, petty encumbrances roll off our backs, making the emotional and mental load a lot lighter. As cancer survivors, Suzanne and Jenny know they have enough to deal with, and they are indeed dealing with it. Everything else is small potatoes.

Oh, potatoes…don't mention those to Suzanne or Jenny. They ate a lot of those during their diets.

1/14: GAIL

One mark of a true friendship is the ability to "pick up where we left off." I guess I've always known Gail and I do just that, but it wasn't until she spoke it that I fully realized it.

Indeed, we do. It had been several months since we spent time together, but in the grand scheme of our friendship, it was the blink of an eye. Gail married one of my husband's best friends, his roommate before his circle of bachelor friends began succumbing to the lure of marriage, one by one. We both had two boys not far apart in age and spent time together as couples and families.

Sometimes real life allows husband and wife to live happily ever after, sometimes not. I know they did all they could, but she and her husband did not stay married. My husband and I have done all we could to keep them both as friends. I think we have done a good job and she agrees.

Her lunch choice was a downtown coffee shop. She spoke openly but only briefly about the heartache and heartbreak one endures because of divorce, but more importantly, she focuses on the peace and happiness she has found since.

On days such as this gray and cold January day, we both agree that such peace and happiness can be hard to keep in the forefront of our minds. Gail and I are in "The Club"; she too is an adult orphan. Her father died on Christmas morning after an extended illness just three years ago, and her mother died several years before that after waging a brave battle against cancer. We always understood each other from the start, now we are bonded by this commonality, something nobody wants to identify with.

We lick our wounds and focus on the future. We both agree that a weekend, or even a single day getaway, is in order for us. We acknowledge that, even before our losses, January is the loneliest, darkest month for both of us. The holidays were over again, and while we both enjoyed a mostly sweet but little bit bitter Christmas with our families, we needed each other's company for at least a full day.

This day would come to pass five Saturdays later, when we would leave our four boys with my husband—he was very willing—and travel to Hays, Kansas, just 100 miles west on Interstate 70, and home of my alma mater, Fort Hays State University. I knew all the old and new haunts, restaurants, and shopping spots there, so we made it a date. It was just what the doctor ordered, but I am getting ahead of myself.

We left after a splendid salad (for her) and a tasty sandwich (on my plate) and headed up "The Hill" in our small city to show off my new office to her. On the way, we would drive by her workplace, an office that is home to the software company she markets. She made herself at home in my office, just as I hoped she would. She has a knack for making the best of whatever circumstances she finds herself in, which is why she turned our topic of discussion to an old and overlooked glitch in our friendship.

Divorces between couples in one's circle of friends don't come without fallout, and this was no different. I hadn't thought much about it after it passed, but it was still heavy on her kind heart, so we dug it up, and then buried it forever. I have learned from this ride we call life that such weights need to be lifted in order to fully enjoy the trip.

I know deep in my heart that Gail and I will always be able to stay close, no matter what may arise. I treasure her friendship and her dedication to making the most of life and appreciating the people in it. I'm so glad I'm one of the people in *her* life.

GAIL'S LUNCH DATE

Before I opened my office, there were two people who sought out my professional services for a private consultation to remedy a speech problem. These two people bolstered my faith in my potential to draw clients as a therapist on my own. If these two sought me out without me going to them first, perhaps there were others. If not for these two people, I may not have had enough faith to give it a shot. One of them was Deanna.

Deanna called me. We were already acquainted through Gail, and through our sons' playing baseball on the same team. She told me she had this little problem with her speech, and it bothered her.

Now, if you spend any time with me at all, you will soon realize that I can spot a speech problem from a mile away. Years of listening for and remedying such problems have given me a keen ear for any form of speech impairment. It is what I do. I assured Deanna that her speech was fine, and it was surely in her head. She continued to assert there was a problem. I agreed to meet her to discuss her perceived problem. I was confident that I could dispel her silly little notion in nothing flat. We agreed to meet at Moka's—it seems I have ended up at this coffee shop/bistro many times with my dates.

We found a corner table. She faced the wall, and I listened. I was prepared with a variation of, *"It's all in your head,"* because I had heard her talk many times, and she didn't have a problem. But I did hear her little problem. It was with one word: *"Gail."* It seemed that any word rhyming with Gail—hail, mail, pail—wasn't produced with the right vowel sound. It was minor, but we cleaned it up right there. Easy fix.

It seems hers and Gail's relationship needed not so much a fix, but a little refresher. Deanna and Gail met each other in 2007 as mutual football moms on their sons' teams. They recognized each other as potential friends and started their relationship with lunch. Both would experience divorce, and found their commonalities made them perfect friends at the perfect times in each other's lives, but these tough times did bring about a few dry spots. Gail knew it was time for them to have lunch again. She reached out to Deanna to fulfill her pay-it-forward lunch obligation and broke the drought. It would become a turning point in their friendship.

Because my short-term memory doesn't always encode new information, I sometimes forget events in my recent past that I really shouldn't. I choose to blame it on my children. They are defenseless scapegoats, and this excuse seems to fly with anyone who has ever had children. This memory lapse, however, was resolved when I got to know Deanna. I will apologize to my children right here: It really isn't your fault, but it works.

Here's what happened: There were infrequent times in my career as a speech therapist when a parent would enlist my help outside of the school or hospital setting where I worked to provide individual attention for their child's speech problem. About ten years ago, a woman called me to do just that. I have no recollection of how she found me, but she did. I met her and worked briefly with her son. Our interactions were very professional, and the need for her son's remediation was short-lived. In the throes of raising two young boys, I mostly forgot all about it. This woman, I do remember, was tall, stunningly beautiful and very kindhearted. This woman was Deanna.

As I age, I prefer to stay at home versus going out for social events. I host a large girl's night at my house every year, but this means that the attendees have to "go out." Gail tells me that Deanna feels the same way about going out. I had that party last weekend at my house. Gail also tells me that because it was my party, and I invited her, Deanna came, even though she would have rather stayed home. She came with Gail. It's not like she felt sorry for me, apparently, I have plenty of friends. She simply wanted to honor my invitation to her.

Gail tells me she herself is amazed at how I keep so many friends throughout my life. I ask her if perhaps everyone else doesn't do the same. Apparently not. I am glad I kept Gail, and I am glad Gail and Deanna kept each other. If Deanna has a spot for just one more friend, I'd like to fill it, because I'd like to keep her too. I haven't done a very good job of keeping in touch since our baseball days, and I really want to do better. I think perhaps Gail and I should take our little day trip again to break the spell of winter, and I think Deanna should come along.

1/21: KELLY

I had a lunch date planned for today. Her name is Carolyn, but you will have to wait to meet her. She is a former neighbor, someone I need to spend more time with, but several hours before our lunch date she called to tell me her daughter came home from school sick. Our date was not meant to be—at least not this week.

Lucky for me, I have backups. I let several local friends know that in a pinch, I may be calling on them to have lunch sooner rather than later. Today, I did just that.

Talk about local—she lives just a mile down the road from me. In the rural sense, we are neighbors. We both live north of our small city; she lives five miles from the interstate on the edge of town, I live another mile north of her. The best part of our date today is the timing: Her birthday is in two days. Even though we are celebrating tomorrow—my mother's birthday—I am thrilled to take her out for a birthday lunch. She is reaching a milestone birthday—49. Just like Tina, I believe her. Just like Tina is really 39, Kelly will really be 49.

We didn't always know we were neighbors. We met through Stacy (August 22nd) and her husband four years ago after we had been here for nine years; they had been living in their home for two years. I've always enjoyed our rural neighborhood, now I like it even more.

Kelly is an artist of sorts. She draws pictures of kitchens. She conceives the design and brings it to life inside other's homes. I would love to have her design my kitchen, but, alas, it was designed just 13 short years ago—by Stacy's husband. Perhaps a renovation will be in the stars in the next few years. She is extremely talented, hard-working, and demands nothing less than excellence from herself and others. Usually she gets it—especially from herself. However, she knows, and I know she is not doing what her heart is telling her to do. The problem at this time in her life is that, she tells me, she's not sure exactly what her heart is saying. It's telling her something, but she's not sure what. I am here to help her listen to its whispers, and perhaps its screams. I've heard my own before; I am familiar with the sound. I am trying to tell her what it sounds like.

Kelly's talents are multi-faceted: she is a kitchen designer, a gifted cook, an interior decorator, and an organizer to the nth degree. I dream of being a fraction of the woman she is in these respects. I know, however, that we all have our own gifts. I am trying to tease out the writer inside of me; I hope she is coming through right now as I write.

I have no doubt that Kelly will soon find that something she is searching for deep within.

While she continues to search, she—unknowingly—is helping me discover another passion lying dormant inside me.

Kelly was there within a few hours after my life hit the wall. She brought food—homemade chicken noodle soup for the body *and* the soul. My boys would have gone without that night if not for her, because my husband was sick with the flu, and I couldn't even sequence something as simple as making a sandwich for them in the hours after I got the news about my parents. She has always been a gifted cook; she kept this soup frozen for just this kind of need.

She continued to carry me through the long weeks and months after life returned to "normal." After two years of the "new normal," I read a book on living through grief, which involved undertaking a project requiring that I build and decorate an actual birdhouse. In order to show that something broken can indeed be made beautiful again, her artistic abilities surfaced once again in another form: she taught me how to engage in mosaic art. I have always been visually and aesthetically drawn to this art form, and I had no idea that I was able to create something so beautiful. The outside of my birdhouse is covered in broken but beautiful ceramic and glass pieces, as well as small trinkets and other meaningful small objects.

I have gone on to create other pieces, and I will be forever grateful for her influence. She says it fills her up inside too, and we laugh now because when we are in someone else's house, we look around at their breakables and imagine how good certain pieces would look if we could just break them and use them for art.

Perhaps these similarities stem from the fact that we both began our lives with the initials K.A.K., both married M.D.s (a Mark and a Mike, not doctors), thus both becoming K.A.D. Perhaps not. I think that is simply icing on the cake.

You see, as a friend of Kelly's, you not only get to have your cake *and* eat it too, it comes smothered in delicious icing. It's the full meal deal, both in her kitchen and as her friend. I know deep in my heart she is the kind of friend I'll keep, even if she does move nine hours away to greener pastures. She will indeed, but just like Amy (July 13th) who already lives in her new city, distance won't matter with this kind of friendship.

KELLY'S LUNCH DATE

So, I am only seven lunch dates into my project, and I am already bending the rules. After much nagging—she won't deny this—she finally decided upon her lunch date plan. Except that it really wasn't a lunch date, and it wasn't just with one person. Kelly paid it forward with a very special married couple from her high school days—on the phone.

Kelly did move away. Nine long hours away from me, after being about one minute away from me. She moved to Minneapolis, Minnesota, accepting an offer she couldn't refuse. No one who knows Kelly would disagree with this: Kelly is not happy if she isn't continuously challenged with a career that stretches her limits—the limits of her time, energy and creativity. She found that in Minneapolis. A lucky design firm lured her there to manage their facility, open a new showroom, and take their company to heights no one there had ever known. But enough about her professional abilities. That's not what this is about, but it helps tell the story.

If Kelly isn't *busy* (one of my least favorite attributes in myself, so I rarely can call myself *busy*), then something is wrong. Or is it right? I have lectured her on this madness she continues to sign up for, and she knows she makes herself *too* busy sometimes. She is well aware of this, so hopefully by putting it in print, it will serve as a reminder to her to slow down. She treasures her parents, and moving away from them has, perhaps, made her more aware of the gift they are to her.

Mr. and Mrs. Sheahon were substitute parents during long periods of time in the summers between her high school years. Kelly played baseball with a traveling team, and she had to stay away from home during the summers in order to be part of the team. Mr. and Mrs. Sheahon took her in when she was away, and they were just who she needed when her parents couldn't be there. Too much time had passed since she had let them know her appreciation for all they had done for her so long ago, so she saw this as the perfect opportunity to connect with them again. She knew it had been too long, and they welcomed her heartfelt call.

She may not have called them otherwise, so, in this case, bending the rules was the perfect plan.

I'm all about bending rules that don't necessarily serve anyone's best interests. Obviously, Kelly is too. Yet another reason I like her so much.

1/28: CAROLYN

Carolyn chose to dine at Gutierrez Mexican Restaurant, my favorite in our small city. She is so agreeable and doesn't even know it. She has so many other virtues that she is unaware of, which is probably the reason why I was drawn to her when I met her about ten years ago as my neighbor. Until exactly one year ago, she lived just across the highway from me. Succumbing to the high level of activity her children were involved in within our small city, they finally decided to move into town to avoid the frequent trips that consumed so much time, energy and fuel.

I miss Carolyn and her family. As can be expected, we didn't see each other as much after they moved. I didn't make enough effort. I am making an effort today.

Carolyn's two boys are near the ages of mine, and her daughter is a few years younger. Another commonality we have is that she is a runner. That is, until she struggled with injuries, then discovered a unique passion: fencing. She and her boys have been competing across the country in fencing tournaments and placing at or near the top. She tells me today that her husband has gotten his feet wet in this sport, with her daughter as the only holdout. There is a local fencing club they belong to; it has been in existence for only a few years.

Her passion for fencing is perhaps the only aspect of her personality that is competitive or confrontational. Every other element of her personality is in accord with her work as a healer and caregiver. Carolyn is a physician at our local Veterans Administration (VA) Clinic. She now works part-time taking care of the men and women who have taken care of our country. She takes great pride in this opportunity to give back because that is her nature.

Her previous position came into conflict with her kind and gentle nature and her family values by the fact that she had to work grueling doctor's hours without the control she needed over her caseload or schedule. She knew in her heart this wasn't allowing her to be the wife, mother and human being she was meant to be.

On a personal level, I can offer you another story that further illustrates this. On June 2nd, 2007, Carolyn and I, along with five other women over 40, hiked the Grand Canyon from top to bottom and back in one day. *(Don't try this.)*

We started out together at 4:30 am, stayed together until the bottom, but then broke off in groups of three, one and three according to our residual energy levels. I was in the last group of three with Carolyn. My friend Shari—you will meet her on April 8th—and I struggled, but not as much as Carolyn. She appeared to be diminishing much faster than we were with several miles still to go, so we took another break. We each carried a backpack with water and food, and we took them off to take a rest. Carolyn laid down on the picnic table, and when she asked me to get her something out of her bag, I gladly did so. When I picked up her bag, it all made sense. Being the healer and caregiver, she had packed her bag full of every conceivable medical supply she could fit in to be prepared for any injury or emergency that one of us might experience. Her bag weighed three times as much as anyone else's, and she had been bearing that weight all the way down, and almost all the way back up. Shari and I took turns carrying the bag from that point, and we carried Carolyn—so to speak—the rest of the way up with jokes, laughter and even singing. We drug our exhausted bodies out of the Grand Canyon at 6:30 pm, fourteen hours after we started, and a full hour after the first group of three.

From the depths of grief to the depths of the Grand Canyon, I know Carolyn will always be there for me, carrying whatever weight and pain she can bear, so that my load may be lessened. I hope and pray that I can be aware and sensitive enough to her needs to repay her at least in some small way if she ever needs me.

When Carolyn came to visit me several months ago, she brought me a refrigerator magnet that reads: "Wag More, Bark Less." As a lover of dogs, she knows how important this is not just for dogs, but for humans, too. If the whole world would wag as much as Carolyn does, and bark as little as she does, it would be a much better place.

CAROLYN'S LUNCH DATE

When Carolyn was a physician at the private clinic, she organized a lunch for the local female physicians. Dr. N. was one of her guests; she was a physician at the local Veterans Administration Clinic. She told Carolyn about the opening for a physician at the VA clinic, and the rest, as they say, is history.

Dr. N. has since moved an hour east to Manhattan, Kansas, and serves as the medical director of the Traumatic Brain Injury Clinic at Fort Riley, an Army base near Junction City, Kansas. She has a son and a daughter who is in her residency to be a physician.

Appropriately, they had lunch on Veterans Day—they both had the day off. They dined at Wood Fashion Café, where four of my other lunch dates and I dined. They talked about work, Carolyn reports. I know that Carolyn cannot talk about something like the work she does now without injecting her optimism and hope for a better future for our Veterans. I'm sure if I asked Dr. N., she would report that Carolyn spoke of seeing the good among all the sadness and brokenness she works with every day.

When I was writing her lunch date story, I found an envelope tucked into my notebook. Carolyn had given it to me on our lunch date, and there was a profound poem inside she copied by hand for me. On the envelope were these three lines she wrote herself:

Everything in life, good or bad,
happens with a purpose.
Sometimes if we're lucky, the reasons are revealed.

I know this; I've known it for a long time. It simply took a reminder from Carolyn to make it come to life. I don't know Dr. N., but I'm pretty sure she was placed in Carolyn's path for an obvious reason.

I have worked with several patients with head injuries, but no soldiers. I bow down to Dr. N. and her mission to make their lives as whole again as possible. There are no heroes more deserving of a normal life than our veterans and active-duty military.

2/17: NANCY

If Nancy were still my boss, it might appear that I was trying to gain favor by treating her to lunch, but she's not my boss anymore. It has been 12 years since she was my supervisor. I was a speech therapist in the school setting, and she was never a "boss" in the superior sense of the word. She was above us in ranking, yes, but she was one of us, a group of 16 therapists who served the schools in this area. She was a boss anyone would be happy to have. If she wasn't, I wouldn't be taking her out to lunch today.

My first lunch date on December 1st was long overdue, but not quite as overdue as this one: It was almost three years ago that I uttered the words, "We should have lunch." Obviously, we never did—until now. I didn't maintain contact with Nancy after I spoke those words. I know she understood. She called me several days after my parents died, offering support and friendship. She always had a sense of what others needed at the right time. This time was no different, except that she has now made this kind of caring her life's work. She retired several years before that phone call and has become an ordained minister in her church. She is perfectly suited to bring comfort and peace to others as a spiritual messenger, but she does it on such a human level. I knew the passage of those few years wouldn't diminish her sincerity, and I knew she would still understand the place where I was and have evolved to. She's "in the club" too.

Nancy is married with a 31-year-old daughter who is a practicing forensic psychologist in San Francisco. She visits her every few months because, like me, she knows life is too short. Her son was taken in a car accident almost eleven years ago when he was 18 years old.

Nancy and I speak of the pain that was, and the joy that can be found after such a loss. It only takes several words to acknowledge that; the grief is always there. We both know it becomes manageable, and with faith, grace, time and effort, there is so much happiness to be found after such a loss.

It is the natural order to bury one's parents. It is not the natural order to say goodbye to your child as they depart before you. As I do with anyone who has lost a child, I bow down to her. I have no idea what she is going through.

I recall going to her son's visitation the night before the funeral. It was just several weeks after my second son was born. This new bond I had just formed was the same bond she had to let go of, and I couldn't bear the thought. I didn't have the words for her then that she has for me today and had for me just after my parents died.

I realize now, after all, we *are* both speech therapists, and words are our lives. She always did have this gift, both professionally and personally. She was my supervisor as well as my teacher, having agreed to the one-year commitment that every newly minted speech therapist must establish and maintain with an experienced professional: The one-year clinical fellowship period of supervision necessary before a permanent license is issued. She really didn't have much choice; if she wanted me to work for her, she would have to supervise me. I had both a pulse *and* a temporary license, and speech therapists with any level of experience were hard to come by in 1994.

We meet today at Carlos O'Kelly's, a local Mexican restaurant—her choice. Ironically, I worked here when I was in graduate school studying to be a speech therapist.

Our conversation flows easily, but it is not the same breed of conversation we used to have. We don't talk shop; we have bigger fish to fry today. She speaks of her work as a minister, and she lights up from deep inside. She has a natural glow about her as most redheaded women do, but this goes deeper than her skin. She has found her calling. I understand this. We both spent time in a satisfying and worthwhile career of words, but a deeper vocation lay in waiting for both of us. We have both heeded the call. She is extending her love of the spoken word, using it for the spiritual benefit of her congregation. I am furthering my passion for the written word with this book, hopefully benefitting the reader with a sense of the value of time and relationships.

She, too, knows the value of the written word, and she tells me today about the notebook she has started in her church. It is a record of "good works;" each member of the congregation who feels they have shared God's grace to someone else is encouraged to write it in the book, anonymously or otherwise.

Ah, words. They are the currency of Nancy's and my work, the human exchange, and God's work, too. There are graces that cannot be shared without them. We both know words—spoken and written clearly and with meaning—are a gift from God. Our words today reflect that.

My journey of words as a speech therapist began many years ago with Nancy. Today, my journey through life after loss is made even brighter with her words.

NANCY'S LUNCH DATE

You would think I had already learned the "life is short" lesson well. Obviously, I did not yet fully appreciate this fact. Nancy sent me a story about her date via email on August 1st. I read it, kept it in my in-box, but didn't follow up personally with her. It was a wonderful story; she got hers written before I had mine written about our date. *Finally,* almost a year after our date, I perfected our lunch date story and sent it to her. She sent back an email the next day, greeting me casually, and thanking me for the story and for the date. Only after extending her greetings and well wishes, did she tell me her news: She had recently been diagnosed with breast cancer. It was very aggressive.

In typical Nancy fashion, she went on to tell me of her upcoming intensive treatment, all the while keeping it very positive.

I waited too long. I knew better. Now Nancy was very ill. Again, you would think I had already learned this lesson. (Refer back to the first line of this book.)

I carried a gift for Nancy around in my car for several weeks. Finally, after running into a mutual former co-worker in not just one, but *two* places one afternoon earlier this week, I knew it was time for me to visit her. This was her "good" week, she told me; Nancy was now receiving treatments every other week. I called her; she welcomed me that afternoon. We sat for an hour at the dining room table in her country home just outside our small city.

With Nancy, it is not possible to feel uncomfortable, even if time has passed, and illness has invaded her body. She greeted me at the front door, and I immediately noticed her stylish new hairdo.

"Do you like my new wig? Today is the first day I am wearing it," she said. Truly, I thought it was her own beautiful red head of hair, streaked with a few light markers of age and stress. She would adjust it throughout our visit, laughing and commenting on the new feel of it all, and how she feared the center part was sliding off to one side. It wasn't. Even if it was, it would still have been beautiful. There's no way it couldn't be, even artificial hair on her head is fueled by a beautiful spirit from deep within.

We spoke of life and loss, a common thread in our recent conversations. She remains positive, with her faith guiding her through this unknown territory. Gratitude is a common theme in our discussion today, with both of us agreeing that the simplest things—the sun shining in the window on us—are God's great blessings. We speak of inspirational books we have both read lately, our reading choices underscore our awareness of all there is to be thankful for. One of her favorite new books challenges the reader to make a long gratitude list. She has posed this challenge to her congregation.

"I know I will be okay," she says. "I know that whatever happens, I will be okay." I know this about her, too.

We spoke about the "new okay" in times of uncertainty, and how it will eventually come. We just don't know at this time what that "new okay" will look or feel like.

The sure knowledge that our loved ones are "okay" too—much more "okay" than we are, or than they ever were on earth—-keeps us both in its cradle of faith. Time has healed us both, but time takes away, too. It took too much away from Nancy and her cousin, the woman she chose as her lunch date.

Nancy tells me today about this cousin, the daughter of her mother's sister she had been close to while growing up. They both live in this small city, but it had been five years since they spoke. Not because they were estranged, they were just "busy" (the four-letter 'b' word, in my book). My lunch date challenge has brought them very close again, even though, initially, Nancy said it was "awkward." After that date, Nancy re-established ties with another cousin, her lunch date's brother. He lives in Colorado Springs, and Nancy and her husband saw him again six months ago when they were visiting there. They became even closer as a result of Nancy's illness. She tells me my *52 Lunches* project was the catalyst for these renewed relationships with her cousins. At this point, I can't help but become a little teary with joy and a smidge of pride for bringing these cousins together.

We agree at this point there can be some very positive things that come out of tragedy.

Nancy and I—along with our 53 lunch dates, as well as her male cousin—are living proof.

Nancy chose to write her own narrative about her lunch date.

LUNCH WITH MY COUSIN CHRISTY by Nancy

After calling my cousin, Christy, on the phone, I invited her to have lunch. We had not spoken in five years, not because of any one reason. It's just that, as we all know, time has a way of getting away from us. Time passes and before you know it, it's been a few years since two people have connected again. My cousin and I have always liked each other and have always gotten along well. It's just that we lead two different lives and rarely, if ever, do our paths cross.

Therefore, when I was presented with this idea of having a lunch with someone I needed to see again, Christy came to mind. We talked for about 30 minutes on the phone that day just catching up on events in our lives—our husbands, our daughters, our mothers, our work. I was excited when she called me back telling me she was ready to set a date for our lunch together.

We met at Applebee's. We began our conversation where we had left off on the previous day. Things are always easy with Christy. I feel that I've known her my whole life which, by the way, I have! We've never been extremely close but are always able to catch up like this from time to time and feel like we've never lost a beat.

During this conversation we again talked about family issues. We still had five years of 'stuff' to talk about. Conversation began easily. Again, it focused on family. Family is always a good topic for a conversation because there's always a lot to discuss. That holds especially true with Christy since our mothers were sisters and we had that connection with each other already.

Christy explained the health problems that she had endured this past year and how she was not able to work for much of the year. I felt bad that I didn't know anything about this. I, as not only her cousin and friend, but also as a pastor, would have liked to have been there for her through the long series of procedures that she had to endure. I wish I had known. It seems that God tugs at my heart when people I know are ailing or are in need of a little compassion. I felt God telling me to call Christy and make her my choice for this special lunch date. I am so glad I did.

I told Christy about the 'pay it forward' concept of the lunch. She readily agreed to take someone else out for lunch in the near future. Our lunch date ended as we vowed to keep in touch better in the years to come. I certainly hope that's true! I have very few close family members left. This meeting taught me that I need to demonstrate the appreciation that I have for the ones remaining. I think that we get so caught up in the everyday humdrum of life that we forget why we are here on this earth. As Jesus explains over and over again in the Gospels, we are to love others. This life is way too short to not spend at least some of it with our close friends and family demonstrating that love.

3/3: CHRISTY

December 1st has not always been an Independence Day for me. December 1st, 2004 was a bittersweet day. After six months of luxuriating in my own private office at the hospital where I worked, my new co-worker was starting on this date, and we would now share what once was my very own space. I wasn't sure if I could share; I had become territorial. The bitter turned sweet in short order when she arrived. In no time, I began to miss her when she was gone. Ours was previously a one-woman staff before she came, and I needed the help. For those six months before she came and after her predecessor left, I worked overtime just to get the basics done—the paperwork was always piled up and waited.

I left her on March 16th, 2007, after only a little over two years together. I still miss her, and I don't see her enough, so I made her my lunch date today. We dined at a mutually decided-upon Mexican restaurant—La Fiesta.

Christy has a wonderful and uninhibited ability to call a spade a spade, and let the rest roll off her back. I have taken that cue from her because I know now that life is too short to get uptight about most anything.

Today, her announcement takes me by huge surprise: She is now ready to leave the hospital, with another job waiting. I am happy for her. The change was good for me, and I can sense that it will be good for her, too. She will go to work in our local school system, the same one I started my career in, the same one I met Nancy (February 17th) in.

She has a brilliant mind for this profession, and a personality that allows others to see that brilliance without her having to point it out—not that she ever would; she is too humble. She is a friend first, and a former co-worker second. She is always a colleague I can call to access professional wisdom greater than my own when the need arises.

But that's only the beginning. Since she arrived on December 1st, she has enhanced my perceptions of so many other things besides professional knowledge. She dwarfs me by about six inches, but she always sees things on my level.

If I could give you only one example of her kindness, it would be this: At 10:00 am on March 5th, 2008, just hours after the news of my parents' deaths hit, she was at my door. She took time off from work— my previous employment— and drove the 20 minutes from her house to mine with her preschool daughter in tow, to offer me two angels. Two angels that would represent the two angels that now looked down on me from above. I will *never* forget this kindness. Not even if I grow old and develop dementia, just like so many of the patients she and I treated at the hospital. I will *always* remember this kindness on the darkest Morning After in my life.

Christy is married with a grade-school-age son, as well as her daughter. Her daughter is her "Million Dollar Baby," because that is what it cost to keep her alive when she was born a bit early with multiple complications. She is healthy and thriving now. Somehow, I think this experience heightened her sense of empathy when others experience a loss, even though she was able to hang on to her daughter.

As I mentioned in the introduction, this project is primarily a demonstration of gratitude, but secondarily, it is a tribute to the gift of one's ability to chew, swallow and enjoy "normal" food and liquid. About half of the patients we treated at the hospital in our time together were not able to do this. Perhaps it is this shared work experience, perhaps it is the laughter that makes it memorable, but I have to share this fitting story from our days together:

We were behind the closed door in our office. Because we went to the same university, we had yet another thing in common: we could share stories—good and bad—about our former acquaintances there. While I had a mouthful of water, Christy told me something *so funny* about one of them. I couldn't help but inhale half of the water in my mouth. In our profession, we call this *aspiration*, and it is never a good thing. It is what we aim to prevent with every swallowing patient we treat.

I coughed hard and then coughed some more. When I was able to breathe again and try to talk—my voice was tight because my vocal cords were doing their job of contracting to try to keep the water out of my lungs—my laughter became an expression of pain. My chest hurt worse than I could ever remember and continued to hurt all day. I recall this episode when a patient coughs and appears to be aspirating. I do my best to treat them and prevent it from happening again, and I think *I know how you feel.* Then, I chuckle a little at myself, and at the memory of the laughter we shared before I aspirated a dangerous amount of water. Christy still makes me laugh when we are together, and I love that about her. I am careful now not to have a mouthful of water when she does.

CHRISTY'S LUNCH DATE

Christina paid me one of the best professional and personal compliments I will ever receive: after she completed her student internship with me, she told me that the most important thing she learned from me is that some rules need to be broken, and when—as well as how—to break them. I will treasure those words from her forever. She included them in her lunch date story (July 22nd).

Since I am the sole proprietor of this project, I can make my own rules, I can break them, I can change them, and I can break them again. Many of them needed to be broken and/or changed. I set out with the intention that each lunch date had to stretch in their reach to connect with someone, and, preferably, all these "someones" shouldn't be duplicated. I changed that rule. I let Christy's lunch date be one of my lunch dates.

I love Christy. I adore Christy. I respect Christy, personally and professionally. I am jealous of Christy. Christy moved to Colorado.

After she spent two years working in the area schools as a speech therapist, she, too, heeded the call and headed west, as did another young woman in my book: my lunch date, and now her lunch date—Christina.

Christy and Christina live 20 minutes apart; Christina in Fort Collins, and Christy in Milliken, Colorado. Christy and Christina had the pleasure of getting to know each other at the hospital in our small city when Christina completed her internship there. Now, living as close as they did to each other *here,* they rarely see each other *there.* They had to make a date to do it, and Christy's fulfillment of her pay it forward lunch date was the impetus for the date.

They met at Rock Bottom, a local brew-pub. Fort Collins is a mecca for breweries, and they took advantage of that for their date. I could have guessed this, but Christy tells me they spent a considerable amount of time talking about how much they both love Colorado, and how much they *don't* miss our small city, or their previous work situations. Of course, they both still miss *me*. She invited me, and just as soon as I get this down on paper, I am packing. I can't take it anymore. *The mountains are calling, and I must go.*

Because Christy and I are experts at communication—its science, its mechanics, its pathologies and its repair—we communicate quite well. It only took a phone call on my way home from work to gather this information; she painted the picture with words. I can see the two of them dining, talking, reminiscing. It's all there. She paid it forward very well. They connected again, and that is the name of this game.

**

Christy and I treated hundreds of patients in our time at the hospital. There are a handful neither of us will ever forget. I told her about one of them, who, not long ago, I paid a visit to. J.P. was ailing, weaker than when we stopped therapy. My heart broke for J.P., and I knew Christy's would, too. Still, it was good to see him, and I called Christy to let her know about my visit. She was glad to hear I had visited with him; it had been too long, too many drives past his office without stopping when I knew I should. I was glad, too, glad I listened to that little voice that told me *JUST STOP ALREADY! STOP DRIVING BY, AND JUST STOP!* It had ceased to be a little voice at that point, it was now a jab in the side, a scream in my ear. It was time. I knew this was a rule I shouldn't break.

When I got home after collecting Christy's story on the phone, I opened our daily local paper. J.P.'s obituary was on page three. I called Christy back. Our hearts broke a little, knowing the pain his family would experience, but we both knew the incredible legacy he left behind, and we know that this is the circle of life. We've been here before.

In memory of J.P.

3/9: NANCY

There is an old joke among therapists in the rehabilitation field that goes something like this: "So the occupational therapist says to the physical therapist, 'Yeah, you may be able to get our patient to walk to the door, but I'm the one that gets them to open it.'" I guess the speech therapist would be the one to help them say, "Come in."

Nancy is an occupational therapist, and she opens doors with her warm smile and easygoing manner. I've hosted another therapist named Nancy for lunch lately (March 17th), and throughout this one-year period, you will meet even more therapists. They are all former or current co-workers, supervisors, or colleagues. They are all fondly within my heart.

Prior to my stint at the lone hospital in our small city, I worked at a hospital in the even smaller city of Abilene, Kansas, home of Dwight D. Eisenhower. It is a quaint and historic town, and just down the road from me. Nancy was a full-time occupational therapist, and I was one of two part-time speech therapists.

I enjoyed every minute I worked with her. She is the mother of one son just a bit older than my oldest, so we always had plenty to brag to each other about. I enjoyed the entire staff as well as the job, but the time came to move on. I was privileged to see her working in one of the nursing homes I now covered, as she was filling in there when needed. No matter how much time had passed between our visits, it felt like yesterday.

No life is without struggle, and hers is no different. Since the days we spent together at the hospital, she has endured a difficult divorce. She speaks of the pain of not seeing her son as much as she had hoped. As a busy teenager he now splits his time between both parents, as well as his friends, sports, and other activities. In my attempt to console her, I let her know that I, too, feel my son beginning to pull away from me, even though we are under the same roof. I don't, however, understand the pain of divorce, and I am sure to let her know I am not minimizing that. I simply know the nature of the beast with teenage boys.

There is a very bright spot she speaks of, that being a reunion with a high-school classmate-turned-boyfriend. Her happiness with this relationship radiates from deep within, it is obvious in this short lunch date. I am happy for her. She speaks very hopefully of the future with him, and he is on the same page.

We dined at the local Pizza Hut in Abilene. She orders a small dish from the menu, and I overdo it at the buffet, like I always do. She brought me a small gift bag, and I accept a handmade pair of earrings that are just my style. She is dabbling in the art, she tells me, but to me she already looks like an expert.

We compare notes about our similar upbringings. I didn't know until today that she, too, grew up with six siblings. There were four girls and three boys in her family, the gender split in my family was the opposite. She knows half of the pain of losing parents; her father died when she was 19. In light of my compounded loss, I remind myself that I had almost 42 years with two wonderful parents. She didn't have that with her father. She remains close to her mother. If this isn't the case with a friend, I gently remind her that they may run out of time to resolve old hurts, and perhaps the time is now to do their part to smooth it over. I wouldn't have offered that advice before, but thankfully, Nancy doesn't need it.

Nancy doesn't need much more prompting to get out there and pay her lunch date forward, and she already knows just who it will be. In short order after this date, I received an email from her to let me know that she took a giant step forward in a stalled relationship. She knows life is too short, and she resolved an old hurt with an old friend. I can sense the joy in her message, and I can picture her smile of satisfaction. She reached out to bring peace to an ailing friendship.

NANCY'S LUNCH DATE

I knew Nancy's ex-husband from my work in the hospital in my small city. He is a prosthetics technician, fitting artificial limbs for those in need. His office and workshop are in the basement of the home he and Nancy once shared.

He hired a man to help him part-time, a man who is married to Nancy's good friend. Nancy was hurting from losing her marriage, losing time with her son, as well as her home. This work relationship strained Nancy's friendship with his wife, and these hard feelings caused her to neglect their friendship. This friend went to the Christmas party with her husband, because he was now employed by Nancy's ex-husband. The party was in Nancy's former home. Ouch.

The lunch date was casual, Nancy tells me. She hadn't yet confessed her hard feelings. While they were waiting for their lunch to arrive, Nancy shared a printed copy of the introduction to this book, so her friend could see the big picture behind the project. She already spoke the language. She lost her mother several years ago to Alzheimer's.

I am not surprised at Nancy's approach to the elephant sitting between them at their lunch table. She addressed it as they left the restaurant. Nancy asked for her forgiveness for the strained friendship, stating she had no idea how stressful it must have been for her friend and her husband to suffer through a long period of job struggles. Her friend understood, confirming through tears that it was a great strain, and for job security, he felt he should go to the Christmas party. Being in Nancy's old home was uncomfortable for her, too, but it was his job.

Nancy and her friend have their old friendship back, only stronger. In capital letters in the e-mail she sent describing it, Nancy said, THESE LUNCHES ARE SO IMPORTANT!

This would be the only lunch her friend was treated to throughout her husband's long period of job struggles. When the tides turn, and the time is right, her friend will indeed *pay it forward*. She had already seen the movie, and her life already embodies the essence of the project, so she understands. She *gets* it.

3/12: ILA

I stated in the introduction that it didn't matter much where my lunch date and I ate, or what we ate. Today is an exception. Ila was hungry for shrimp, but because several of her family members were allergic to shellfish, she didn't often have the opportunity to eat it. She was fond of Olive Garden, but her home was about four hours from the nearest one, and when she was close to one, she couldn't convince any of her family members to eat there.

Today, I made it clear to Ila that I wanted her to pick absolutely whatever she wanted to eat, wherever she wanted to eat it. I emphasized that several times, because it was very important to me that she got exactly what she wanted to eat, in whatever restaurant she wanted to eat it in. She may not be back this way again, so to speak, so the Olive Garden it is.

Ila was diagnosed with pancreatic cancer several months ago. She turned 67 years old on the first of this month, and it is my great pleasure to spend about five hours with her today. I had been trying to find a way to have a few hours of her to myself, but I felt too selfish to ask how I could do that. Her family needs her more than I do, and, unfortunately, her time is likely much more precious than mine.

Ila is choosing to spend her time with her four children in their respective homes. Two of her four children live in the Kansas City area, one lives near her home in western Kansas, and the fourth is my dear friend Shelly (April first), who lives just several miles from me in a rural area north of our small city.

Ila was with her daughter near Kansas City, and I happened to be near there, too, arriving the evening before this. She needed a ride to Shelly's house, so I jumped at the chance to share my day with her. She is my friend's mother, and these days, I take motherly companionship whenever I can get it. It's the next best thing.

Her shrimp and pasta dish appeared to be just what the doctor ordered. She savored all that she could consume during lunch and packed the rest up to take with her. As usual, I ate all of mine. I don't miss any meals, and I usually don't have leftovers. It's the waste-not farm girl in me.

The conversation was just as good, if not better than the food. She spoke of knowing that, short of utter defiance of medical odds, her time is short. She is realistically hopeful, knowing that sometimes miracles still happen. She is keenly aware of the elements of her life she wants to change before she passes; she's not denying the difficulty she will likely encounter when trying to set certain things right. She wants peace in her heart and soul as she continues the journey through to the end, whenever it may be.

One of the hardest things I encounter in my work in the nursing home setting is the denial of the obvious. Usually, it is the family of the patient, but sometimes it is the patient themselves. Ila isn't going down that road. She has faith, which often cancels out fear. She isn't willing to give up any of this precious time to denial. She is spending it with her children until she can no longer travel. They will be okay, and in the end, she will be even more okay than they are.

Before I proposed this idea to Ila, I ran it by Shelly to see if she felt her mother would be a willing participant: terms, conditions, and all. She may need help with transportation in order to fulfill her effort to pay it forward, and Shelly is willing to help with that. Shelly thought it was a great idea; Ila agreed. As I write, Shelly and her mother have traveled one hour south of our small city to the home of a high-school classmate of Ila's, just two days after our date. She's clearly not wasting her precious time.

I wasted mine, though. Ila planned to be at Shelly's house on May 1st for her grandson's First Communion. Shelly's son, Luke, was the man of the hour, and Ila wanted to be there to celebrate. I planned to go to Shelly's house that evening to hear about her date in person.

Ila died that morning. I thought I knew how precious time was, but I didn't fully realize it this time. I hadn't seen her since our lunch date. My last memory of her will be a good one; I can picture her enjoying her shrimp, giving me motherly advice and attention, and referring to me as "kid."

So, finally today, August 25th, Shelly and I are enjoying coffee in my cozy office, a long-overdue coffee date that we agreed to have after the kids started school again. She makes herself comfortable while I read her mother's lunch date story to her, and after shedding a few sweet-bitter tears, she tells me about her mother's pay it forward lunch date.

ILA'S LUNCH DATE

Just like I've wanted all my lunch dates to have their pick of restaurants—especially Ila—she, too, wanted her date to have her pick. However, her friend Lois wasn't yet aware that Ila was on a mission. She didn't yet know that Ila's time was limited, and she probably shouldn't waste any time eating at a restaurant she didn't like. Ila wanted Mexican food, but Lois didn't. Without Lois knowing the reason for this visit, they compromised and ate at a local downtown restaurant called the Bread Basket. Lois knew she was being treated to lunch but didn't know why.

Shelly brought her mother to Lois's house, took her to the restaurant and left Ila and Lois alone to enjoy their lunch. Ila related the rest of this story to Shelly after their date.

Lois and Ila had been friends since their freshman year in high school, becoming fast friends when they met over 40 years ago. Lois moved to their small town at that time and recalled that Ila had a "presence" when she walked into the room, describing her as focused and outspoken—in a good way. They had remained friends since that time but hadn't spoken in about six months.

When Ila arrived for this lunch date, Lois was thrilled. However, she wasn't ready. In her pajamas still, Shelly knocked on her door at 11:00 am, just as she was tuning in to *The Young and The Restless*. This was a surprise visit, because she no longer had a home phone, and her cell phone number was a mystery. Set up by her mother—Ila was a practical joker—Shelly posed as an evangelist, telling Lois they wanted to take her to lunch. Lois seemed to think she might recognize Shelly, and Shelly told her she was sure she'd recognize her mother if she'd just come to the car (with Lois still in her pajamas). With a bit of trepidation and skepticism, she made the short walk to the car. The joke worked, and she agreed wholeheartedly to a lunch date.

After a five-minute negotiation, the restaurant was agreed upon, and Shelly took her mother there, followed by Lois. Shelly gave them the time they needed, which was about two hours. They could have likely spent two more hours, both knowing now that this could be their last visit. The news blindsided Lois, but they worked through her feelings of shock enough to make this likely last visit a meaningful and memorable one. Ila was feeling relatively good that day, according to

Shelly. She cannot be sure, but it appeared that her mother stayed strong when she delivered the news, because Shelly can recognize her mother's face and eyes after she has shed tears.

Shelly tells me today she feels it helped her mother through this process to talk about her situation to those who mattered. To simply show up and announce to someone who hasn't been in your life for several years that you are dying shows us all the importance of keeping in close touch with those who do matter to you.

We could all stand to learn this lesson a bit more, myself included. I *would* have gotten the story myself from Ila, I *could* have gotten it earlier, but I didn't. I put it off.

I think, however, Ila has forgiven me.

3/29: ANITA

"Here's to Christy!" we said as we toasted to our mutual friend with our water glasses. Just four weeks ago, I was at this very same Mexican restaurant with Christy—La Fiesta—when she surprised me with news of her decision to move on professionally, just as I had, and just as Anita recently did, too.

Anita is a physician's assistant at our local Veterans Administration Clinic. She now has the privilege of working with Carolyn, who was my January 28th date. She left her position as assistant to the rehabilitation doctor whose patients both Christy and I served at the hospital. We were blessed to work on the same team for several years, but our lives inevitably changed, and we went our own directions.

Now we are celebrating the friendships that remain after this work circle we once revolved around was dissolved. First by me, then by Anita, and now by Christy.

Life, however, is good, and the best is yet to come. Of this, I am sure. I have learned this from hardship and heartbreak; so, too, has Anita.

In so many ways, Anita is a survivor. She began life as a cherished baby when her adoptive parents brought her home shortly after she was born. She was their only child, but has since made contact with several biological siblings, as well as her biological mother. Anita was meant for her adoptive family, just as she was meant to survive the health crisis that changed her from an optimistic, cheerful person, into a woman of indomitable character with an effervescent presence. I can't come up with words strong enough to describe the positive spirit she now exudes.

Just before Christmas of 2006, Anita was diagnosed with breast cancer. I worked with her at the hospital when the news broke, but the hushed word among the staff was that she didn't want to talk about it. So, I didn't. I remember knocking on the door to her small office and, without a word, I slipped a small angel into her hand. She smiled a grateful smile. She didn't speak, and I went on my way. I left the hospital four months later. I regret I wasn't a strong presence for her in her time of need; I didn't know what to do for her. She was there in my time of need, and she knew what to do for me.

Our mutual heartbreaks and subsequent growth and renewal have brought us closer than we ever were when we worked together. We both are able to see that life, despite its upheavals, has the potential to be a wonderful journey. Today, we share that spirit of optimism. It is easy to feel it when you are in Anita's presence.

We speak only briefly of our former lives, the lives we knew when we were both at the hospital. We focus on moving forward, and how we treasure more moments both great and small—even the bittersweet ones too.

Anita will forever embody the attitude that whatever life hands you, it can be made beautiful with acceptance and understanding. She tells me today that her 25-year-old son is gay. It is not what she had expected for her son, but she knows he is happy, and wants that for him more than anything else. In her generous spirit, she wants other parents to know that their children's lifestyles and choices can be accepted and embraced, and they, too, can find happiness and peace, as long as their child is happy.

Anita has a college-age daughter as well, and she shares the trials and tribulations of the coed, a life I lived seemingly a few short years ago—has it really been 23 years for me?

I feel a bond with Anita; it is an unspoken understanding that we are on the same page regarding our hopes and dreams, and our ultimate goal to share this new awareness we have, that being the unshakeable knowledge that there is so much happiness to be found in life if we simply make the effort to reach out to find it. It doesn't always come one's way naturally, sometimes it takes hard work. We both know it's worth the effort.

ANITA'S LUNCH DATE

By virtue of the size of this small city, I am acquainted with some of my lunch dates' lunch dates. Anita's date, Yvonne, is the director of one of the home health offices I provide in-home speech therapy for. She is a small-but-mighty woman, just like Anita, and just like I sometimes call myself.

Yvonne had been called upon to muster more strength than she likely knew she had, but it was there, and she put it to work to save a reputable public agency from demise. Human nature and politics brought this agency to a low point, and Yvonne, at the helm of a ship full of other strong women, brought it back up.

Yvonne and Anita are on the Board of Directors of a local women's group, Women Helping Women. They spearheaded the effort to bring this homegrown charitable organization to fruition, and it has flourished beyond their wildest dreams. I am privileged to be a member of this group, a group who does exactly what its title says: we donate to those women in our community who need a boost to buy new tires, a new washing machine, who need gas to travel to a hospital 100 miles away to spend time with her newborn premature baby, who work hard but can't make it all happen, and can find help nowhere else.

Anita and Yvonne make a lot of things happen, and they do it in their own style. Yvonne, after winning this aforementioned battle, chose to hang it up early, as did her husband in his work. They realized the stress wasn't worth it. They moved three hours east to spend time with their children, who are blended by their subsequent marriages: Their "bonus" children, they call them, the children they each gained by marrying the other. I am now using that term for my own "bonus" son. (December 29th). I love it.

4/1: SHELLY

Two stories, ago, you met Shelly's mother Ila. Today, you are meeting Shelly. We met at a mutually desirable restaurant, a relatively new spot in our small city. Typically, it matters not where we eat, and while it is not as vital to the story as her mother's choice was, it does tell you about her.

This spot on a downtown corner used to be a dry-cleaning business called Wood Fashion Cleaners. The owner changed just one word, and it became *Wood Fashion Café*. They specialize in organic, locally grown food. While I try to eat healthy, my friend Shelly is all over that. They even created a dish just for her. It doesn't appear on the menu, but "The Shelly Bowl" is her namesake. I told her it sounded like a sporting event.

I have known Shelly for about ten years. We may have crossed paths years before that when we attended the same university at the same time, but neither of us remembers if we did. We met because of my name. My first son was in a daycare in a rural setting close to her house, and she was given my name as a reference when she was shopping for a daycare provider for her first newborn son

"I called you because I knew with a name like Depperschmidt, I could trust your opinion," she said when she placed the first call of hundreds (thousands?) to me. My married name is a German masterpiece; she recognized it from her roots in the same part of the state my husband came from. She even had an 'Uncle Paul' Depperschmidt.

We were both busy new mothers, trying to juggle our babies, our jobs and our families, leaving little time for a social life. We tried. We had lunch once and thoroughly enjoyed each other, but we didn't make the time—then.

A chance encounter both of us remember was at our small city's arts festival in early June before my second son was born in late July. She and her husband were pushing their first son in a stroller, and she tells me now, she counted her blessings that it was me and not her in that condition, in that heat.

It would indeed be her in that condition just a few short years later, and she, too, would welcome the arrival of another son. Both of us adjusted our busy schedules to accommodate a new baby, and we found ourselves working more from our respective homes. Another encounter would give us the chance to devise a plan to swap boys once a week, giving each of us one morning every other week to ourselves in order to tend to our businesses in peace. These exchanges began with good intentions, but soon we found ourselves having coffee before we left each other with four boys, and those mornings of liberation were soon traded for an entire morning of good coffee and good companionship between our boys, and especially between us. The plan to take care of business took a backseat to our blossoming friendship. I continue to remain grateful we had the good sense to realize what was most important.

Our lives have changed since then. Our older boys are taller than their mothers, and the younger ones aren't far behind. We have each taken several different career paths since then, but we remain neighbors in the rural sense, and we continue to be bound by the strength an old friendship affords. We both know loss; her father passed away just days before her second son was born. Now that her mother, Ila, is gone, we both know too well the pain of being an adult orphan.

More than the bitter, we focus on the sweet. This pain, this loss that puts us next in line to God, has made us stronger people, and while it is a club no one wants to be in, we find ourselves in it, and we have found peace amidst the emptiness we still feel. We have a long history of sharing joys as well as pain, and while joy is doubled when it is shared, pain is cut in half. That's the beauty of a true friendship, and we both know it.

I think I am the perpetual winner of the "Shelly Bowl."

SHELLY'S DATE

Shelly dined again at *Wood Fashion Café*, just several weeks after our lunch date. Of course, she ordered the "Shelly Bowl." Her date, Mel, had yet to experience this local treasure. I know Mel from a previous short-term work stint; Shelly knows her from the local YMCA. They would frequently cross paths there, but their work schedules have recently changed, and they don't get to see each other as much as they once did.

I mentioned in Shelly's date story that she is very interested in organic food, and in line with that, she is zealous about natural health. She is a wealth of information about natural remedies and cures for many ailments. Unfortunately, Mel needs her advice: Mel's husband struggles with a chronic, but manageable illness, and traditional medicine has offered him little reprieve. Shelly has offered him useful advice, and is she is grateful for that.

Moments prior to my lunch date with Shelly, she was shopping in a downtown store when she ran into Mel. As well as Mel, Shelly was considering many people for her lunch date. When Mel showed up in that same store just before my date with Shelly, she knew Mel was the obvious choice. It would seem—by mutual sentiment—that they have an uncanny knack for running into each other when one or the other has the other one on her mind. They both attest to this. This day was no different, so Mel became the obvious choice.

Mel and Shelly are both busy part-time working mothers. Shelly is a marketing manager for a local laboratory, and Mel is a teacher, so their schedules do not lend themselves easily to lunch dates with each other. They both have children: Shelly's boys are eight and 12; Mel's children are ten, eight, and five. Mel is ten years younger than Shelly, and they have no mutual close friends. Still, in spite of this stretch, Shelly felt the need to connect. Mel agreed.

While waiting for Mel to arrive, Shelly became concerned that perhaps this would not work, as they hadn't verbally confirmed the date. Mel's kids had Bible School that day; it was a busy summer week. Still, it worked. The coolest thing is that they showed up wearing the same necklace—an angel medallion.

My hope for this project is to create a geometric progression, with the second-generation lunch dates continuing to *pay it forward,* and so on. Thus, a never-ending, multiplying phenomenon occurs. A grand dream, I know.

Mel and Shelly recently ran into each other in public weeks after their date. Mel reported this with a big smile: She had already paid it forward not just once, but twice, and shared the story with each of her dates, and asked them to do the same. She has taken it over the top, further than anyone else I know of at this point.

It is now time to weave my past connection to Mel into this story. Ten years ago, I took a trip to Hawaii with my husband. It was an incentive trip. I earned it from the home-based, multi-level business I was involved in. In order to earn it, I had certain individual and "team" sales requirements. Mel was on my "team." I use quotes because I no longer like to speak the language of sales and numbers. It doesn't fit me anymore. I earned the trip and dropped the whole business like the proverbial hot potato. Mel's sales were one of the reasons I went to Hawaii—free.

Five years ago, I ran into Mel while standing in line for coffee at what is now Moka's—the sandwich shop where six of my lunch dates took place. I knew about her third pregnancy, so I asked her when the baby was due. The baby had been born two weeks earlier. I firmly tucked my tail between my legs, offered a weak one-arm hug, and gave her full permission to never speak to me again, if she chose.

Obviously, she didn't hold it against me. Now, five years later, both of us have experienced the struggles life can bring with it, but we both know life goes on, and life can be really, *really* good. We both know the importance of the people in our lives.

Ten years ago, I thanked Mel for her help in sending me to Hawaii. Five years ago, I told her how sorry I was for the apparent insult. Today, for helping me further my *52 Lunches* project, I say to her, "Mahalo."

4/8: SHARI

There are silver friends, and there are gold friends. Then, there are friends who are more precious than the most exquisite diamond. Shari is one of those friends. By virtue of longevity, our friendship is among the most enduring and timeless. Shari and I started kindergarten together in 1971, and while the usual grade-school-girl issues hovered at times, we have grown closer with each passing year.

Shari and I make a concerted effort each year to meet around the time of our birthdays—they are only six weeks apart—in "The Little Apple." Manhattan, Kansas, is home to Kansas State University, Shari's alma mater, and a good geographic middle ground for us to meet. She lives in the Kansas City area, and her humility would prevent you from knowing this unless someone else tells you: She is a brilliant engineer with a national company headquartered there. She holds a leadership position, supervising approximately 150 people.

But that's just business. If there was a way to measure the value of a friend in objective terms as one's salary and position is measured, this measurement would dwarf her job status.

I can tell her anything, I can count on her for sensitive and helpful advice, and here's the best part: Whenever I am with her, I laugh a lot.

She is in the Boys Club, too. She is the mother of a nine-year-old adopted son, and the wife of a fourth-grade teacher. Amidst her 12-hour workdays, she manages to elevate those roles to her highest priorities. She cooks gourmet meals, maintains a tidy home, entertains for family and friends and gardens like a madwoman *after* she spends quality time with her boys. I am not making this up.

It is easy to assume that everyone has a friend like Shari, because she has been a part of me ever since I can remember. Doesn't everyone have a Shari? Doesn't everyone have a heart and lungs? To me, she is as necessary and lifesaving as both organs.

I know how lucky I am. I have lived long enough to see that not many people have a friend like her. If, indeed, the most concise and meaningful definition of loneliness is having no one to share the deepest part of yourself with, then I am exempt from that dark emotion with only her friendship. This is not to take away from the other wonderful people I describe in this book. I simply mean that if I only had her to lean on, then I could survive. Lucky for her I have so many others, and she doesn't need to carry that weight.

We may go for several weeks without talking on the phone, and perhaps as long as six months without seeing each other, but no matter how much time passes, we don't miss a beat. It's that hokey, overused sentiment: we always pick up where we left off.

As part of our annual ritual, we hike the locally famous Konza Prairie Trail, just outside of Manhattan. We meet there first, spend a few hours hiking, then head into the Little Apple for lunch, shopping, and our annual treat—maybe a massage or a pedicure.

Lunch is always the first priority after the hike, and like so many of my other lunch dates, we agree upon Mexican food at Coco Bolo's, a local favorite. It is in Aggieville, an enclave within Manhattan. Aggieville is home to many hangouts—restaurants and bars—and shopping of all kinds. It has a local reputation as *the* hangout hot spot for college students at Kansas State University, but even "old" people like us enjoy it there.

The food is divine, but it's no match for the company. When I am with Shari, I feel a sense of calm and complete acceptance. I can let it all hang out with Shari, and today, I do. We share hopes, dreams, disappointments and joys, mostly joys today. I tend to forget all the other weighty issues when I am with her.

We finish dining and move on to shopping. Shari typically needs coaxing and coaching in order to shop, and she assures me I am just the expert to help her pick out a few new outfits. I think I'm pretty good at shopping, too, so I share my expertise. We find her a few professional outfits, a few fun ones, and she insists on paying for the shirt I find for myself as part of my birthday gift.

Shari's shopping meter expires before mine does; good thing because it is time for our pedicures. We schedule ourselves at the local training academy, partly because they are cheap, but also because the entertainment value is priceless. The students are trained well enough to do a good job on our toes, but no so well refined yet to keep us out of the drama going on in their lives as they work next to each other. We laugh to ourselves and to each other, thanking God we are past that stage in our lives, and thankful, too, that neither of us signed up for their kinds of issues.

If either of us have issues, we don't let them cloud this day. As I type in my office, I am looking at my favorite magnet that reads: *"Cancel my subscription, I don't need your issues."* While I would like to meaningfully speak these words to some people, those words will never come out of my mouth with Shari. As a matter of fact, I hope to continue to renew my subscription year after year with her.

Speaking of subscriptions, one of the Christmas gifts she gives me every year is a subscription to *Real Simple* magazine. I love the magazine, and I love her, too. With her, friendship is just that: *real simple*.

SHARI'S LUNCH DATE

Shari hasn't seen her friend Vikki for about six months. They met as Bible study co-leaders. While I don't know Vikki, I know that if she is Shari's friend, then she, too, lives the lessons in the Bible. Shari tells me Vikki's philosophy of life: *We are all put on this earth to love God and love others.*

I like Vikki already.

Vikki was with Shari in person and in spirit while Shari's son, Luke, was waiting in the womb to join their family, offering her prayers for his safe arrival on this earth and into Shari's family. Her prayers worked. Luke arrived safe and sound and was placed into their arms not long after his birth.

Shari describes Vikki as caring and kind, compassionate and non-judgmental. She accepts them for who they are. She has a certain sweetness about her, Shari says, but she can be firm when necessary. As a Christian, her goal is to learn about Jesus and live her life as close to his as possible.

I have never met Vikki, but I would like to. From what Shari tells me, she sounds very similar to another amazing woman I knew. A woman who was kind, compassionate, accepting, and non-judgmental. A woman who tried—and succeeded—to live a Christian life. A woman who believed we were put here to love others, because that is what she did—especially her children.

That woman was my mother.

4/22: MARK

The first time I laid eyes on my husband, I thought to myself: "Hmm…he looks interesting." He was hurling his long, lean body over a second-story railing onto the ground floor of a bar in our small city. He was clad in a softball player's uniform matching his teammates who surrounded him—on the top floor. I *definitely* wasn't thinking, "I'm going to marry that man someday." This was summer 1989.

It would be several months after that first sighting that I would actually meet this man.

Today, he sits on the side next to me at a square table in Shelly's favorite restaurant, Wood Fashion Café. He had yet to experience dining there, so on this Good Friday, we met for lunch. It was indeed a good Friday. Every Friday—and *almost* every other day with him is a good day.

Just as my first impression suggested, he really *is* an interesting man. Along with that, he is devoted, loving, kind and a whole list of other positive attributes that would probably nauseate you, so I won't go on. Just know that he is the man I said 'Yes' to, and now, almost 17 years and two sons later, I am still glad I said it.

His workday was shortened by the inclement but welcome spring rains, so he is able to devote a leisurely hour-plus to our date. He is a commercial builder, but used his sweat, tears, blood, and brilliance to build the beautiful home we live in.

We rarely go out to lunch together, so this is a treat. We enjoy this restaurant's locally grown organic food, talk about our boys for a few moments, work, and business for just a few more, but then turn the topic to our date. He is honored to be my date today, and thanks me for choosing him not just today, but always. Again, he is a good man who still adores his wife after all this time, and considering the risk of turning your stomach again, I will stop there. Let me just add that he is so much more than interesting, but that is one of the reasons why I still like to hang out with him at home, at lunch, and wherever else we go.

He loves and respects his family—both his parents and siblings, as well as the family he has created. Before I was ever introduced to him, the friend I met him through was quick to point out that yes, he is the classic "nice guy," but perhaps even more important than that, he is such a wonderful father to his then-three-year-old son, Matthew. I treaded carefully, knowing that if we were to date, he would be a package deal with his son, and this was a responsibility I didn't take lightly.

What I have learned along the way with this package called Mark and Matt is this:

1. It's not always going to be about me.

2. A good man can be measured in large part by how he treats his children, and most importantly:

3. Any hardship I ever endured as a stepmother is far eclipsed by the joy a loving man and his son can bring to my life.

Knowing I wanted children someday, I had a built-in barometer of his potential father fitness level by watching him with Matt. It made it much easier to commit to a man when I had this gauge.

I still have this gauge, and I still use it. Our sons Joel and Jude are ten and 13, respectively, and Matt is now 25. They are as close as long-distance brothers can be. Matt lives in Omaha, having graduated from college and working now in "the real world." Mark's devotion to his wife is matched only by his love for his boys. He is an involved, caring, and hands-on father to his sons near and far. My mother told me that I needed a daughter, because they take care of you when you get old. I told her I'll get some good daughters-in-law. Until then, I know these boys will all take good care of me. I joke that as the only female, I am the queen of the house. All four of them treat me accordingly. I am a lucky woman, and I know it.

MARK'S LUNCH DATE

Mark is many things to many people. To me, he is an almost-perfect husband. To our children, he is a pretty cool dad. To his family, he is a devoted, kind and loving son and brother. They have known him the longest, they should know.

Second to the family's record of knowing him since the day he was born are his oldest friends. One of those friends, Cliff, has been his friend since junior high. He was a groomsman in our wedding. He lives with his wife and two teenage daughters about 100 miles away in Wichita. We travel there several times a year; it would be easy to make time to visit him. Except that it hasn't happened in a long time.

Mark and I were going to Wichita to pick up his son, Matt (December 29th), for the Depperschmidt family Christmas celebration. Knowing Cliff may have a lighter schedule from his teaching and coaching responsibilities during Christmas break, I suggested that perhaps Mark should give him a call.

I have heard the stories. Cliff and Mark were in junior high and high school together and, frankly, they scared me (the stories, that is). Knowing that my children have his genes as well as his influences, I wish I hadn't heard the stories. I won't go into detail, but just imagine what two teenage boys can conjure up to entertain themselves in a small town in western Kansas that has many hills and some extra tires lying around in the pre-electronic device days. Oh, and they had access to matches.

Our other two boys and I went along to Wichita. Mark didn't call Cliff; I suggested it, but I didn't persist. It wasn't my deal—at the time. We stopped to shop a bit, which is never long with those three. We found a great lunch spot—Pei Wei's (pronounced pay-ways), which is the faster version of its parent Asian restaurant, P.F. Chang's. We settled into our meal amidst the busy lunch crowd and the hustling waitresses. One of those waitresses caught Mark's attention. Her features reminded him of Cliff.

It had been many years since we saw their daughters, but she was indeed one of Cliff's two daughters. Mark nailed it. It isn't easy for him to approach someone he doesn't know well in this type of situation, but he was sure it was her, and he called her aside as she whizzed by.

"Yes, I am McKenzie," she said. And with that, the "lunch meeting" was fated for this date with her dad and Mark. She called him, and since their house was only several blocks from the restaurant and her dad wasn't busy with anything at the moment, he came there. It was a nice reunion after a too-long respite in their get-togethers. They have always settled easily into each other's company, and today was no different. I watched it: the smiles, the handshakes, the laughs, all which started the updates on their lives at this point, and inevitably the reverie. Always the reverie. That's why old friends are the best—there is history that serves as a bond between old friends, and these two are no different.

Our teenage boys were becoming a bit restless since lunch was over, which was about the time the call came in from Matt: his flight would be about two hours late. Perfect. Perfect for Mark and Cliff because they had two extra hours together. Perfect for the boys because my brother who lives close to the restaurant with his wife and two boys was home and they were, too. Perfect for me because with my three boys farmed out while waiting for the fourth one, I had two extra hours to myself to shop.

Perfect for everyone except Matt, who did make it to the airport two hours later. I picked him up, which gave Mark and Cliff a few extra minutes, and we all met back at my brother's house to claim our respective family members. Cliff and his wife are acquainted with my brother and his family, as both wives are teachers in the same school.

Their "lunch" became a few hours at a nearby sports bar, allowing them to have a few drinks, check out the sporting action on the big screens, and partake of a few appetizers as the time passed. Cliff didn't know he was part of a "project." It would have spoiled the mood if I told him then. The important part is that Mark reached out, not quite in the way I had intended, but by stopping that waitress as she whizzed by.

Life is funny, in the way that we are placed in certain places at certain times with certain people. I don't believe in coincidences, and this was not a "coincidence." This was all about timing, and we nailed it.

Pei it forward.

4/28: VONCEILE

I have been able largely to seek out my own friends, and I think I have made some great choices. Others were presented to me, and I had a choice to adopt them as a friend—or not. By virtue of marrying into the Depperschmidt clan, I have had the pleasure of meeting some wonderful people either by their bloodline, or as a mutual in-law. Vonceile is one of the other women who married into this large, close-knit clan. We became fast friends from day one, but that friendship was taken to new heights when we both found ourselves in "The Club."

It takes a special person to drive two hours to my parents' funeral when that person didn't know them. It takes an even more amazing person to come to the funeral two weeks after burying her own father after his sudden death. Vonceile is both of those people, and so much more.

Vonceile and I are together today by virtue of our mutual decision to marry into this large family. She married Mark's cousin Blaine, with whom she has three children. She lives and works in nearby Lindsborg, the Swedish capital of America. Ironically, we dine today at this small town's only Mexican restaurant.

Thursday is her day off, which is why I called her only several hours before this date when my scheduled lunch date couldn't make it. I can count on her to bend her day-off plans just enough to fit me in. I thank her for this, but no need; she is unruffled. She was only doing laundry, she says. One of the many things I like about her is that she lets the small stuff slide, and she is not afraid to speak up in order to change the big stuff when the need arises.

Vonceile is employed part-time by a financial analyst in her town. Because our lunch conversation naturally evolves towards the "Life is Too Short" topic, she shares this story with me from her job:

Her boss, without seeking her prior approval, began to expect her to work longer hours by assigning her more projects. She quickly realized the direction this was going and brought it to his attention. In no uncertain terms, she let him know that she was employed part-time for good reason. Three good reasons, actually—her children. They were growing up whether she was at home or at work, and her oldest would be gone from home in just three years. She wouldn't stand for it. He saw the light and relented.

All of us learn life lessons the hard way from experience. Someone can tell us what we need to know about how to live life and savor every moment, but most of us don't listen until this lesson is rubbed in our faces. Her mother learned that lesson in just that manner, and Vonceile tells me the story today. I hadn't heard it before.

Her mother's mother wasn't feeling well and asked her daughter—Vonceile's mom—to come to her home that evening. She replied that with her busy household—she had four children at that time—and well, she was just too busy. So sorry, she told her, she would come over tomorrow.

Tomorrow didn't come for Vonceile's grandmother. She died that night. Vonceile never met her grandmother; her own mother was in her thirties at that time, and Vonceile was born late in her childbearing years.

Vonceile's mother never forgot that lesson and has done all she can to impress it upon her own children. They, too, learned the hard way, when their father died sitting in his favorite chair after a brief, seemingly mild illness. This is why Vonceile understands the language of grief no one wants to speak until you find yourself there in that foreign country, just as we have.

Because I told you from the beginning that this book was not a downer, I will end this story as such. We finish our lunch and step out into the beautiful spring day. The vibrant green leaves of spring adorn the small trees planted in cement squares evenly on the Main Street sidewalk, and the birds sing in the calm breeze.

"Life is good," I affirm, as I give her a goodbye hug.

"Yes, it is." We need not say anything else. We both know how lucky we still are.

VONCEILE'S DATE

Sometimes friendships fizzle because of a falling out, a misunderstanding or lack of attention. Sometimes, they just fade away. That is what happened to Kim and Vonceile.

They were best friends in high school: "We did everything together," Vonceile said.

Kim now lives about three hours east of Vonceile in Olathe, a suburb of Kansas City. After finding her on Facebook, Kim and Vonceile met in the middle—geographically—in Lawrence, Kansas.

"I might have done it someday, but I had no plans to get together with her. I decided she was the one I needed to connect with."

Kim has a son, and was recently married, but not to his father, who was her high school sweetheart. Kim is a cancer survivor, and obviously knows how to take care of herself—and her son.

"It was like no time had passed," Vonceile said. "We laughed like the old days, and we have been in touch since."

5/4: KELLEY

Today, I paid my respects and honored the life of Ila. I am spending five of my 24 hours of this beautiful day on Interstate 70, traveling to tiny Park, Kansas, to celebrate her life. She passed away with her daughter Una at her side four days ago. Her daughter Shelly, whom you met on April 1st, has been there for me through thin and thick ever since my parents died, and today I want to give her most of this day. I hang around like an invited and well-tolerated third wheel, and I am thankful to be part of the after-the-funeral tears, laughter, business, and reverie.

Around five o'clock, I offer whatever measures of support I can to the family, and I hit the road. Just 25 miles down the road, I have a "lunch" date waiting. This will be the first lunch-turned-dinner date; I couldn't work it out any other way.

WaKeeney, Kansas, is home to about 2,000 people, none of whom I know. Ness City, Kansas, however, is just thirty minutes south, and home to my dear friend Kelley. She has agreed to meet me here along Interstate 70 on my way home.

Kelley and I met in college (Go Fort Hays Tigers!), and I'm glad we made the connection. Our friendship has stood the test of time and distance, because it wasn't until two years ago that she returned to Kansas from the Dallas area to allow her husband to jump-start her farmer father's retirement by taking over the family farm. She has capably assumed the role of high-school secretary, where her daughter attends as a junior. Her son is in the fifth grade.

Our dining options are limited here: it is between the authentic Mexican restaurant or the authentic Chinese restaurant. The latter choice is ruled out when we read the cardboard sign on the door: "We are closed for six weeks because of a 'dead' in the family." They may not get our language perfect, but they sure understand the language of loss: They take six weeks off when a family member dies. They know what it's about. Perhaps we should take a cue from them.

So Mexican it is, and we slide easily into a booth and even easier into conversation at El Dos de Oros. We catch up on each other's growing children and show off their pictures proudly as peacocks. We wonder where the last five (six? seven?) years have gone since we last saw each other and chalk it up to time flying. She marvels at this book idea; I blush. She always was full of compliments, deserved or not. She tells me she needed such a kick in the pants to get past some big issues and hang-ups that are getting smaller after putting them into perspective when I sent her the introduction. So, I gave her the kick—so to speak—and we marvel at how great life really can be, and usually is, for both of us. We talk about how quickly life can change, but how we have the faith and strength to bounce back.

Kelley was there for me from a distance when my parents died, and I will never forget what she wrote in the card she sent. While there are no words to make the pain go away, grief can be lightened a bit when it is shared. There were so many caring people who carried me through those dark days. Kelley, along with two other friends, helped carry the burden in a heartfelt way with the same words they personally wrote in their cards: "My heart breaks for you." I will never forget those words, nor will I forget the kindness of the three friends that wrote them. No other words written in the 150+ cards I received went straight to my heart as those five words did. She has never walked in these shoes, but she knows how to make the walk just a bit more bearable. Today, she doesn't have to speak it, but I know she will always be there to help me through any more darkness in the future. I hope she doesn't ever need me, but I would do the same for her.

We revisit mutual friendships we made in college, relish the wonderful parents we were both blessed with, and talk about our younger sisters who, coincidentally, both live in Osborne, Kansas, where my parents lived. Kelley has no brothers, just one sister.

We joke about how easy life was in college, how carefree our days were. Neither of us, though, would go back. We know how blessed we are to have our faith, our families, our health, our jobs and, especially today, we realize how important friendships are.

I still have two more hours to drive before I sleep; I wish we had all night. Our long dinner isn't enough time to make up for several years of lost time. We vow to get together sooner rather than later, perhaps we can coordinate a visit to our sisters at the same time. I know the hard way that life is short and uncertain. She didn't need to learn this the hard way, she already knows it. We will see each other soon. Of this, I'm sure.

KELLEY'S LUNCH DATE—as written by Kelley

This has been a wonderful year for me. You see, I was blessed to have celebrated another birthday. Now, this one's no ordinary birthday; I turned 50!!!!!!!! I realize some of you (probably most of you) are groaning, thinking she has lost her cotton-pickin' mind! I must tell you I am one of the very few who looked forward to being 50. You see, for me it was quite liberating, having spent most of my life trying to please everyone. At the ripe age of 50, I had an enlightening moment. I no longer really cared about what other people thought of me; or rather I wasn't trying as hard to be anything other than me.

In reflecting on my life thus far, I have realized many things had changed, including friendships. When my sweet friend, Kathleen, asked me to lunch and told me of her idea for a book, I was inspired by her passion. Although she and I had not seen each other in quite some time, ours is a friendship that can pick up right where it left off. Her eyes sparkled and her voice was laced with excitement as she talked about her idea and the importance of slowing down to enjoy the things that we so often take for granted, I don't think intentionally, but we always think "one of these days." I also think that the older we become (or perhaps it's just me), the friendships we have are different than in our younger days. I know I have become selective as to who comes in my inner circle. I don't like to think of it as being cynical, but rather understanding those who are the kind who will be there for the long haul—the good, the bad and the really ugly.

Of course, I wanted to jump aboard the adventure and so with a promise (now three years old) to Kathleen, I set out to find the one who would help me fulfill my commitment and also pay it forward. Now, life has a funny way of giving you unexpected surprises along the journey, and I had the great fortune to have a long-lost friend find me.

I am one of those people who believe that God sends us others for a reason. Some pass through our lives for a short period of time, and then there are the ones you think of often and pray the good Lord will keep safe, healthy and happy. My friend Stacey is one of the latter.

I met Stacey while in college. I was living in an apartment below his brother-and sister-in-law. He came for a visit, and I guess you could say we hit it off. He was quite the charmer, with blond hair, beautiful eyes and a smile that could light up a room. We were both very young and had the whole world in front of us.

We hung out a few times and then as fate would have it, we moved in different directions. He got a job, got married and became a first-time dad. I moved to Texas, got married and eventually became a mom. He called me once while I was in Texas and we visited about our kids, and at that time he had just added boy #2. It was so good to hear from him; little did I know we would eventually see each other again many years down the road.

Fate stepped in once again and totally changed the life I had planned. My family and I moved back to Kansas (this was not in my plans), back to my hometown, to begin our next journey. At that time, Stacey was working for a company that brought him through my little town once in a while, and eventually we met for lunch.

I was very nervous to see him again, I mean, let's think about this: it had been well over 20 years, a few more pounds and a few gray hairs (actually, a lot of gray hair), so I was quite sure the image we both had of each other might be a wee bit different.

Stacey was just like I remembered: beautiful eyes and a wonderful smile. We laughed a lot, talked about the "old college days," and I had to give him a hard time for "breaking my heart," which we always laugh about. We talked about our families—he is now the father of three boys and one grandson—and things we have been up to over the years. He is passionate about his family, and he lights up when he talks about them. He has a great job that still has him traveling a bit of the state, but he enjoys it. His sons played on the high school golf team (and I believe all are state champions), and I found out he used to keep track of me through our high school golf team, asking a few of my students what I was up to. Of course, I had to tell them not to believe everything Stacey had to say! It was such a wonderful time catching up on everything. Stacey is one of those friends who I may not see or talk to very often, but yet I know he is there, and we can pick up right where we left off.

I am truly blessed and thankful to have a friendship with Stacey, and I smile when I think of him. My heart is full with thankfulness that he was one of the people God sent me to leave footprints on my heart.

5/13: SHARON

I am not superstitious, but I *did* run out of gas at a busy intersection in my college town on a Friday the 13th. Several years later I went on to graduate from that college on a subsequent Friday the 13th, followed by four years of gypsy-style living while trying to put my sociology degree to work. I thought, perhaps, that it was bad luck, but after returning to college for my career degree, I find myself feeling lucky to be a sociologist first. That is in part what drove me to embark upon this project.

Today is another Friday the 13th. I feel lucky today because I am having lunch with Sharon. We are dining at Speakeasy, a classy bar and grill with a brilliant name that I wish I'd got to first for my business, so to speak. (My business, coincidentally, is called So To Speak.)

Sharon and I do speak easily, as we have for years—about 40 years, actually. Sharon and I grew up in the same small town; our parents were close friends. Sharon and my sister, Gail (you will meet her on July 2nd), were in the same class, and I am six years younger. Gail always had the coolest friends, and while none of them were mean to me, I know I was the annoying little sister when they were hanging out at my house. Of all of her friends, I remember Sharon treating me the nicest.

Sharon drives the few blocks from work at the bank to meet me here. Just like so many other lunch dates I have had or will have, we always said, "We should do lunch sometime!" We are doing it today.

Sharon and I, along with Christy (March 3rd), were all employed at the hospital together at one time. Sharon was employed in the Human Relations Department, while Christy and I were both speech therapists. We lunched together at the hospital from time to time, and off the clock, the four of us took part in a Pilates class together. We now have to make dates to get together. It used to be so easy when we worked under the same roof. Time moves on, and we all moved on for the better—except for this aspect.

Sharon reads music and plays the piano like a maestro. She is married with one teenage daughter, Carly, who is also gifted musically. Carly knows she has a gift and plans to use it professionally for the rest of her life. She also plans to marry Justin Bieber. Now don't laugh, because she inherited the qualities that just might get her there from her mother: 1. She has a charismatic personality. 2. She *is* phenomenally talented. 3. She is stunningly beautiful but has no idea.

Sharon's parents—Edgar and Alice—and my parents were lifelong friends. After my parents passed away, my younger sister, Suzanne (December 28th), and I were reflecting on their beloved place in their small-town community—even though they had moved from the farm into Suzanne's small town nearby.

"I can't say the word that describes them in Tipton," Suzanne said. "They were like an Edgar and Alice."

"Icons?" I said.

"Yes, they were *icons.* Just like Edgar and Alice still are," Suzanne said.

Suzanne and I—as well as three of our other siblings—ought to know. The five of us were classmates with five of Edgar and Alice's nine children, and we spent many hours, days and evenings enjoying each other's company in our respective homes. Edgar and Alice produced an amazing bunch of kids—just like our parents did.

Sharon's sister, LeeAnne, and I were classmates. LeeAnne now lives in Colorado, but she was there in spirit on the telephone just two days after my parents died. She reflected on the great memories we made in our younger years on our farm, and I will be forever grateful for her kindness and sympathy from a distance. Sharon was at the funeral. Like several hundred other people, I am so thankful to them for their heartfelt support. They loved my parents, too—just like my siblings and I love Edgar and Alice.

SHARON'S LUNCH DATE—as told by Sharon

My pay-it-forward lunch was with a dear friend, Therese. As I sit here thinking, Therese and Kathleen remind me so much of each other: Beautiful, positive, generous, great sense of humor and full of a high-spirited energy that makes you want to be a better person—just by spending a few minutes in their presence.

So, I have to start with Kathleen because I am kind of a chronological kind of girl, and Kathleen came first in my life. I was introduced to Kathleen's family at a very early age. Her mom and dad were best friends with my parents, and her sister, Gail, was one of my best friends and classmates growing up. Gail and I are still close friends. Just wish we lived closer to each other. I remember the Saturday evenings that our parents would get together and play cards or go to dances or simply go grab a bite to eat. But what I remember most are the trips to the Ketter farm.

When I was a very young age, our family would hop in the car and take a drive west, usually on a Saturday evening or Sunday afternoon. The first part of the trip included the amazing "roller coaster hills" and the thrill of the drive up and down, and that crazy feeling I got in my tummy when we made it up the steepest hill and were heading down. Once over that hill and on our way down, I remember seeing the curve to the left and that meant we were seconds away from the farm. Seconds away from a family that welcomed us with open arms and just let us become part of their day…no matter what time, no matter what day. Mom and Dad would walk in the front door and begin visiting with Ed and Liz. Us kids…we would be off and running in several different directions. Some would head up to the barn to see the new kittens, others would hop on the mini-bike, and some would venture off into the hills. My brothers would often climb up on the tractors in the garage and pretend to be farmers. Endless games of tag or "Run, Sheep, Run" or Hide and Seek out in the yard and fun times in the girls' bedroom telling all sorts of secrets.

Gail and I went on to college after high school and a few years later so did Kathleen. We all eventually got married and had families of our own. Years passed and as Kathleen told you in our story…we got reacquainted when I came to work at the same hospital she was working at. Kathleen so graciously started inviting us to some of her and her husband's holiday gatherings. I loved attending them. Wonderful food, wonderful people and some great memories have occurred at Kathleen and Mark's little spot north of town. There is a calmness and peacefulness I feel when I spend time at Kathleen's home…kind of takes me back to a similar feeling I used to have after heading home from our visits at her mom and dad's farm years ago. Her kindness and generosity and humor remind me so much of her lovely mother, Liz, and little does she know that every Saturday and Sunday morning when I am sitting down having my morning cup of coffee, I always wish I were sitting on Kathleen's porch just north of town...maybe in a rocking chair right next to her, just enjoying the sun coming up over the hills and talking about whatever the breeze just happens to blow our way.

Now—on to my pay-it-forward lunch date with my very dear friend, Therese. I am guessing Therese and I met when I was 19 or so. After a few short months in college, I decided I needed to experience life and go wherever my heart took me. I would describe them as my "gypsy" years. Following the beat of my own drum...my drum led me to work in a music store. I loved music and thought it was the perfect match for me. I got to help people pick out music, introduce them to new artists and, most importantly, got to listen to music all day long! Selling albums, cassettes, 45s and maybe even a few 8-track tapes! Yes, I am dating myself! Therese was the assistant manager of that store. She was smart, funny, and everyone loved her. She made work not seem like work at all. She would talk to every customer, and her knowledge of music was astounding. I learned a great deal from her and soon we became friends. We moved into an apartment together and our friendship began.

Shortly after we moved in together, Therese became ill and struggled with never-ending pain, especially in the winter months. Her bones ached like she was 90. I remember many nights of her being curled up in a ball on the couch with blankets, just trying to keep warm and wishing the pain would go away. It took several months to diagnose, and many trips to different facilities, but finally she was diagnosed with lupus. Therese remained so positive and battled the disease. Her faith was amazing. She would try different medicines. Some would work, some wouldn't.

I got to know Therese's family during the time we lived together. Her parents lived in the same town, and they took me in with open arms, like I was one of their own, and believe me, they had plenty of their own! Therese and I would go over maybe once a week and just visit with her brother, Johnnie, her mom and dad and her grandma. Her older sisters and brothers would come back occasionally on weekends, and they would have family gatherings and, always, Ron and Mary would include me in the festivities. I felt so fortunate to be included in Therese's family.

Therese continued to battle the illness, but she wouldn't let it stop her or bring her down. She always had a smile on her face and continued to live life. She got engaged when we were living together and married within the next year and began her new life. I moved on...actually to several different cities and several different jobs continuing my "gypsy" travels. Eventually, I married and started a family of my own. And yes, many years later, I ended up moving back to the same town where Therese and I met, which also happens to be my husband's hometown.

After we got settled in, I kept telling myself, *I need to call Therese. I need to meet her for lunch.* I would see her every now and then at the grocery store or at the annual river festival and we would always spend half an hour chatting and we both would say, "We need to do lunch, or we need to start taking walks," but we never did. People come in and out of our lives and I knew I needed Therese back in my life. So...when Kathleen shared her book idea with me, I knew Therese had to be my lunch date. And we had lunch at the Speakeasy, the same place Kathleen and I had lunch. It was wonderful to sit and visit. She had gone through remission and had been lupus-free for several years. She was even the leader of a local support group. Her faith is even stronger than before, and she always brings everything back to God. What would God want me to do? How would God view this? What direction is God sending me?

What an amazing, incredible woman; my friend Therese. I have made a promise to keep her in my life. Years had passed, but sitting there, eating lunch, and chatting away...it felt like just yesterday we were sitting in our kitchen in our little two-bedroom apartment, on our lunch break together, and she was making the main course—her awesome chili dogs and chips from the bag for a side!

5/25: ABIGAIL

I am a godmother to several wonderful nieces. Abigail belongs to my sister, Gail (thus, the name), whom you will meet on July 2nd. "Abby," as she prefers to be called, is driving to her mother's house from the Kansas City Airport today and is passing right through my small city on Interstate 70. My younger brother—her uncle Ryan—is getting married in three days.

She flew in from northern Michigan, where she works as a massage therapist/clinic manager. She is 25 years old and is getting married herself on July 27th in beautiful Hawaii. "Mahalo," I say to her, in return for granting me one hour of her precious time on her six-hour car ride to her mother's house. This is lunch Number 26, the halfway mark. It is also the only lunch where we are graced with the presence of an invited third wheel. Her fiancé is along for trip, and because I'd rather bend my rules a bit than ask him to sit at another table, he joins us for lunch.

An easy favorite among many of my lunch dates is Mexican food, and today is no different. *El Atoron* is along Interstate 70 on the edge of Salina as they pass through; it is a perfect meeting place. I am on the road after two home health visits, so we meet there.

It has been a year and a half since I have seen Abby; our last visit was at her sister Kate's (November 18th) wedding in December of 2009. Time flies, but it has been way too long. I have never traveled to Michigan, but I know I need to. The mountains of northern Michigan are beautiful, they tell me. I won't get to see the mountains of Hawaii in July when they take the plunge, so I need to think about committing to a trip to see her at home soon.

I can only hope and pray I am setting a positive example as her godmother. She doesn't need guidance now, and I don't offer it. If she ever did, I hope I gave her what she needed. She has told me I am a positive influence; I hope she's not padding the story.

Abby was born on August 2nd, 1986, just several weeks before I left for an adventurous semester on a college exchange program (see July 29th) at a small university in New Mexico. I could tell you that as the newly appointed godmother, I whispered godmotherly things into this beautiful baby's ear before I left, telling her that someday she, too, would leave on an adventure just like her Aunt Kathleen, but I didn't do that. I was too scared of leaving the familiar to formulate such a coherent wish. More accurately, I will tell you this baby was born with a spirited sense of adventure, a sense that the world didn't have to be seen through the same lens that most people view it through. She has often shifted her perspective in positive directions, enabling her to take in other sights and taste other flavors that most people are too timid to consider.

She tapped into this spirit several years ago when a friend proposed this idea to her: *Move north to Michigan with me. I need a roommate, and you need a break.* So, she did. She packed, moved, went back to school to become a massage therapist, became a manager, and became engaged—in that order.

If it sounds that simple, I know she had her share of struggles before and during the transition. She followed her own North Star to Michigan and found her way from there.

I like to think I possess a spirit of adventure, even if my days of adventure travels are over. I am planted here in the middle of Kansas, but I don't want to be anywhere else. Like Abby, I know I march to the proverbial different drummer. I think, perhaps, there are days when each of us has an entire marching band parading through our heads. I wouldn't have it any other way, and I'm glad she understands her crazy Aunt Kathleen, because she's signed up for the same ride I did.

I looked up the translation of our restaurant's name: "*El Atoron*" in Spanish means something along the lines of "taken captive," or "trapped." There was a time in my life I felt stuck, even captive to my situation and circumstances. No longer am I captive, and it's no place I want to find myself in ever again (except for this fabulous restaurant, and in a later visit, the staff would tell me that is exactly the meaning they want to impress upon their customers). I wish the same for my godchild, but as long as she allows her free spirit to roam, she won't need it. I don't need to whisper—or to speak loudly—any godmotherly things to her. She already knows them all.

ABBY'S LUNCH DATE

When I was 25 years old like Abby is now, I was nowhere near as together as she is. I had just returned from a year away (see July 13th), and I was spending time with Mr. Wrong. I already was acquainted with Mr. Right, I just didn't know it. I even chose Mr. Wrong over Mr. Right when faced with a decision. Thank God I wised up, and Mr. Right took me back.

That is, until he didn't. We had a brief separation, during which time I decided to get my life together and go back to college. (We would eventually sign up for happily ever after.) All this happened in good time, it just took the Godmother a bit longer than the Goddaughter. I would go on to marry at age 28 and give birth to my first son at age 31.

Abby's lunch date needed her company in more ways than one. She came to Michigan at the behest of her friend, Mary, but they hadn't stayed as close as they once were after Mary got married. Abby knew they needed to see each other. They now needed each other more than ever.

Mary found Mr. Right in Michigan just like Abby did and married him. Her happily ever after consisted of trying to start a family, but she suffered several miscarriages. Unfortunately, Abby's ever after was destined down that same road.

I have learned from my own loss that, until you have suffered a particular breed of loss, you don't speak or understand the language. I am so blessed to not know that particular language, but I know that loss is loss, and when it happens, we need to be surrounded by others who understand. Both Abby and Mary speak that dreadful breed of the language of loss.

Abby called Mary after too many months of not being in contact, and they welcomed each other for a visit with open arms. Their hearts were open, too, cracked wide open from the pain, but their recent history—as well as their more ancient history as friends—provided them with a new foundation from which to grow their friendship even stronger.

They enjoyed a lunch that day and have remained in closer touch. Friends in need do need friends who understand, even if they are a friend in need, too.

Abby's losses would break her heart—as well as her husband's, too—but it is not in the Ketter girl nature to stay down too long. Just like her mother, Abby bounced back with faith in her future as a parent and will deliver a child in about five months.

Epilogue: Abby did deliver a bouncing baby boy, and then another one a few years after that. Mary was able to deliver a child in time as well. They remain close.

6/7: KANDY

I spoke in the introduction of the traveling therapist's baton I passed on in January. It had been in my possession nearly four years. Prior to that, I worked as one of the two full-time speech therapists at our local hospital for three years. Several months before I decided to leave the hospital, I felt a stirring deep inside, a little voice that told me it was time to move on. Turns out it was the voice of wisdom.

I began to explore other options. One choice that is typically available for therapists is to work in the long-term care (a.k.a. nursing home) circuit. There is usually a need for therapists. It was less glamorous, uncertain in terms of amount of work, but nonetheless an option.

I called my friend Kandy. She was the baton master at the time, managing therapy programs at numerous facilities in this area of Kansas. She was trying to expand a few programs, and there was a need for speech therapy in several facilities. Nothing was guaranteed: it would depend upon patient load and flow, as well as my ability to identify new patients in need. I knew I had to take it. It didn't make sense on paper or in a rational person's mind—who needed a guaranteed income—but I took it, nonetheless.

This job change took me to a nursing facility in Osborne, Kansas. My parents lived there. Because of this job, I got to see them another dozen-plus times in their last year—I stopped to see them *every time* I was in their town. I knew immediately after they died why I took that job. Kandy knew, too. She is "in the club."

Kandy had three sons. Her middle son, Eric, died in a car accident when he was 17. She knows how important it is to listen when that little voice speaks. I will be forever grateful to her for giving me the opportunity to have those visits to cherish. Without them, my guilt from my "busy" days would have consumed me after it was too late to make an effort to see my parents more. I thank God I was given the gift of another chance. I thank Kandy for being the bearer of that gift. I wish

I could repay her, but she doesn't expect any form of repayment. She only wants me to *pay it forward*.

We dine today at Chili's, a local franchise eatery. We enjoy our food—we're both good eaters—but more than that, we enjoy each other's company, as usual. We laugh a lot, too—as usual. We even made jokes about death. If you're not "in the club," too, I don't expect you to understand how we could laugh about it. If you are, then you get it.

Just like Shari's story (April 8th), we laugh at my favorite message on a favorite new magnet in my office: "Cancel my subscription, because I don't need your issues." I love this. Kandy and I have no plans to ever cancel our subscriptions to each other's friendship.

Kandy would return to Florida soon after our visit, where she has recently relocated and works for the same company. For a time, she continued to manage the facilities here, while sharing her time in Florida with other facilities in the same capacity. Now, she works only in Florida. She would continue this work for just several more weeks after this lunch date, when she did, in effect, *cancel her subscription*. When her blood pressure reached 211/108, and her pulse was 202, she knew it was time. She took herself to the Emergency Room when, at work, she knew something wasn't right on this particularly stressful day. She had had enough of this treadmill, and she stepped gracefully off, calling her boss from the ER to inform her that she was finished, and her health was more important than her job. This had been a long-time coming, and Kandy was tired of all the *issues*.

She lives now with her husband and her mother in a large house in Jacksonville, Florida. She begs me to bring my boys to visit. She knows boys, and she loves mine, too—the big one and the smaller ones. I have never been to Florida. I hope to make our visit my first there.

Kandy once lived about 20 minutes from me. Now she lives on the Florida coast. I don't worry about losing touch with her, she won't allow that, and I won't, either. Kandy was on the phone within 20 minutes after the news of my parents' deaths spread. She has been there for me ever since.

KANDY'S LUNCH DATES

Once again, I am allowing myself to break my own rules. Each of my lunch dates was to have their own lunch date with someone they needed to connect with. Just one, that's all I asked. Without trying, Kandy—once again—went beyond and above the call.

A group of seven other high school classmates had tried unsuccessfully for years to persuade her to join them for an annual getaway to beautiful Breckenridge, Colorado. The parents of her classmate Belinda live there, and the seven others would make the trip for a week to join Belinda and her parents every summer they could. While Kandy did go to the 25th class reunion, she hadn't joined them as a group since then. She did see Suzy—one of the seven—at her son's funeral, but it had been way too many years since she had seen the others. She wouldn't commit, but they didn't give up. This year, at the 44-year mark, she would finally join them. Perhaps the gentle prompt I gave her through *52 Lunches* was the catalyst. I like to think so, and she tells me it *is* so. Sometimes, even after a loss of her magnitude, we all need reminding that life is indeed too short. Perhaps, after her loss, it was just easier to stay home. I get that, too.

So, Kandy's "lunch date" wasn't really a lunch date, it was much more than that. She connected with four long-time friends for a period of days, not just a lunch. In their original group of eight, one has already passed away. Two others were unable to come to Colorado this year because of health issues. That left Kandy with Belinda, Suzy, Jana, and Barbara. I could see from the pictures just how much fun they really had. Trust me when I tell you that they were having the time of their lives.

6/14: LIBBY

When I was a kid, I kept track of how I spent every birthday. From the time I knew how special birthdays were, until I was about 22, I made a point to bank birthday memories. After that, they didn't seem to matter as much.

I do remember my 29th birthday. I worked as a school-based speech therapist, and I had the pleasure of being a guest in Libby's preschool classroom on a regular basis. Libby's birthday was the day before mine. This particular year, we were both enrolled in an evening sign language class, and we had class the night of my birthday. It was a bummer to be in class, until Libby and I were serenaded by a musically gifted teenage boy named Nick, Libby's son. I have a picture of Nick on one knee in front of me, singing "Happy Birthday." I am blushing red, and Libby is laughing next to us. I treasure that picture.

Libby and I dine this fine summer day at Moka's; it seems my lunch dates and I are regulars here now. We pick a bar-height table in the window, a fitting metaphor for two women who want to be in the light as well as in a high place. We have both been in low, dark places in our lives in the not-so-distant past.

There are things spoken to us that perhaps we have heard a thousand times before, but for some reason, it sticks when it comes from a certain person. When I was expecting my first son, I saw Libby regularly in her preschool. She doted on the baby I was carrying, and on me as well. She reminisced about the days when her children were younger and spoke these words I have recalled many times since then, even though I have heard them from so many other people: "In the blink of an eye, they will be grown up." For whatever reason, I carried those words long after I carried babies. I watched it happen as my boys grew so big and so fast, always hearing her voice speak those words.

Those words from her come racing back to me frequently now, reminding me to savor *every single day* I have with my children. My boys are both bigger than I am now, and the eye-blink is almost finished. They will soon be on their own.

We reminisce about our preschool days together. She still teaches, but at a different school. We fast-forward to the present, appreciating the newly found and hard-earned strength we both had to develop. Libby is no stranger to loss, experiencing her own breed of pain and heartache that forever changes a person, but at the same time, makes them savor the smallest tastes of happiness when they are found.

We part ways today and agree on one sure thing: In spite of the heartbreak that life can bring, life *really is* good.

LIBBY'S LUNCH DATE

One theory regarding the human female phenomenon of telling her hairdresser too much is this: Through her work, the hairdresser has to touch the woman gently on her head, and this touch forms a comforting bond between the woman and the hairdresser.

I get this. I think perhaps this is why I tell my hairdresser (almost) everything. In fact, I had hoped to make her one of my lunch dates, but I had to nix her from the list because I see her every three weeks or so, and I bumped her for someone else whom I rarely get to see. She still loves me—at least she says she does. Her name is Sharolyn, and if you need a hairdresser in my small city, I highly recommend her. While I don't know Libby's lunch date as a hairdresser, I am sure she would be a highly competent choice as well.

Apparently, Libby doesn't get enough time to tell her hairdresser (almost) everything when she is in her chair, because she paid her lunch date forward with her at a cozy Italian restaurant in the downtown of our small city. I think it goes a little deeper than that. Marlene, like Libby, has an indomitable sense of fortitude and faith; life and loss have taught her how to develop it.

Libby and Marlene know their own breed of pain; they know about the abyss that remains inside. I know only of a different void, a dark place that everyone expects to go to at some time in their lives when they must tell their parents *goodbye*. I have told my hairdresser everything about this loss. She still has her parents, and I know she treasures them. I don't need to remind her of that. She knows that day will come, and she will let them go as we all must.

Libby is a gifted piano player and teacher, having taught Marlene's daughter how to play as a child. They met each other through their children's mutual activities 15 years ago, and Marlene has now been cutting her hair for 12 years.

"I get my hair cut more than I need to," Libby said.

They share more than spoken words or the heartbreak of loss. Libby is a spiritual Hercules; her faith continues to carry her through the dark days that still come to all of us who have suffered loss. Marlene's faith moves her forward, and when she can't move forward during those dark moments, she leans on it until she can.

I don't know Marlene, but knowing what I know about loss, about Libby and about hairdressers in general, I *do* know this for sure: The gifts of strength and joy Libby shares with her friends are as moving as the power of her faith, the promise of hope for brighter days ahead after loss, and the healing and powerful touch given by a hairdresser.

6/18: MARILYN

It is fair to say that without Marilyn's influence, you would not be reading this book. While there are so many people who have inspired me throughout this journey of words, I must back up to the day I decided to take the path I took before this one.

It was a frigid December day a few days before Christmas in 1991. My now-husband Mark (April 22nd) and I had split, my "career" consisted of waiting tables and doing temp work, and my nights and days were both dark. In the midst of my despair, my stars and planets aligned, and I made the decision to return to college for a master's degree. I became a student again eight months later, and I never looked back. I married Mark the week after I graduated.

Marilyn was my potluck roommate in the dorm when I landed at Fort Hays State University in Hays, Kansas, in August of 1984 as a starry-eyed 18-year-old freshman. She would prove to be a keeper, inspiring me through her zealous endeavors in this field.

I graduated four years later with a bachelor's degree in sociology. While I continue to apply this degree more to my personal life as I age, I couldn't easily apply it in the work world. Thus, the waitress and temp positions.

Marilyn was enrolled as a speech pathology major, and I maintained a curious interest in her field throughout our two years as roommates, and the subsequent years after that as friends. It required a master's degree, however, and I knew I would be lucky to graduate with a bachelor's degree. Those four years between my degrees would prove to be a field study in sociology, ultimately leading me back to the classroom. I now see the world through the sharply focused lens of a sociologist, as I help others to maximize their communication abilities. This trifecta of sociology, speech pathology and writing is my professional *and* personal jackpot. I am blessed.

We dine today at Shorty Small's, a fine establishment on the west side of Wichita, down the road from her home just outside of town.

She lives with her husband and four children, fixing speech problems large and small as a school-based therapist. She moonlights—like many therapists do—in the nursing home as well. Young and old, she covers the gamut.

I always did and still marvel at her ability to let issues large and small roll off her back, never clouding her sunny disposition. Even an issue as small as taking off one's makeup before bed could be dismissed without consequence; I think she may still have some left on her face from 1986, and yet her skin is as pure as the driven snow. You will meet Denise on October 3rd, and Tracy on November 20th. They can attest as roommates—the four of us lived together for one year—that she is the only person we know who can pull this off. Is it going too far to tell you that she could even get dressed for class before she went to bed the night before, literally roll out of bed and out the door and still look like a million bucks? Perhaps I shouldn't divulge that secret about her, but it is to her credit as the carefree, yet caring and responsible woman she is.

We recall those carefree days today but savor the freedom that the responsibilities of parenting and working allow us. We talk only briefly of our work; we seem to be able to communicate with each other about that with only a few words, knowing what the other is thinking on any subject within our field.

We have bigger fish to fry than talking about work. Our families have always been paramount in our lives, with each of us spending a considerable number of weekends on each other's farms during our college years. Her parents and five siblings are all well and close, and she has come to know my brother and his family in Wichita from mutual associations within their communities, even in that big city.

Marilyn was there with Denise and Tracy at my parents' funeral: none of them would dream of missing it. Marilyn picked up Denise in her minivan, the same minivan she was driving several months after our date when, coincidentally, my brother's son in Wichita made an illegal turn and caused her to run into his car. Neither vehicle survived, but Marilyn and her passenger son, as well as my nephew, were without a scratch.

There were no hard feelings; it went no further when it was said and done. It is now simply a bygone, because Marilyn and her family know deep in their hearts that the people in our lives, and how we interact with them, determines the level of happiness in our hearts.

Marilyn is dear to my heart; she has been since August of 1984, and she will continue to occupy a space no one else can: I feel an infinite sense of gratitude for her guidance, and for the sheer coincidence of me being placed in her dorm room. I don't think these things are coincidences, though; I think she would agree there is something greater at work here.

MARILYN'S LUNCH DATE

Marilyn did indeed have her date. She made an effort to get together with a cousin she needed to reconnect with. She asked her out, they had a grand time, she didn't write it down right away, I didn't follow up right away, she suffered a fall in the months following and had a head injury, and the writing of her lunch date story became unimportant.

What is important is that she is now doing okay. Like so many of her patients, she struggled with the symptoms of a head injury: poor memory, mental overstimulation, confusion, fatigue, and disorientation, to name a few. She recovered slowly but surely and was able to return to work part-time after a few weeks. In her classic humorous and linguistically clever way, she described her recovery like this: *"It felt like I was drunk and hung over at the same time."*

She has always been one who understands others, but now, after her head injury, she has a sharply focused awareness of what it feels like to be the patient who struggles, instead of the therapist who tries to help them through the struggles. She still has her infectious laugh and bright smile, she still has her warm wit and effervescent personality, which can be lost after such an injury but not for her—thank God. Those are her calling cards. When I think of Marilyn, I picture her smiling and laughing; that is simply who she is.

Thank you, God, for Marilyn. I don't know who, or what I would be without her.

7/2: GAIL

I knew a woman who was kind, intelligent, caring, generous, hard-working, insightful, selfless, inspirational, and optimistic in a quiet way. I know another woman who has all these qualities in a very open, outgoing way. The first woman was my mother. The second woman is my older sister, Gail.

I am the middle sister of three, and now that Mom is gone, Gail has become the self-appointed matriarch of our family. She had big shoes to fill, and she is filling them well. She and my younger sister, Suzanne (December 29th), have simultaneously anchored and uplifted me—just like Mom used to. I don't know what I would do without either of them.

As I mentioned in the introduction, the inspiration for this book began on the way home from Thanksgiving at Gail's house. It has become the premier fall event in our family, and even though some family members can't always make it because of obligations to in-laws, we all try to be present for this gala. To let you know just how impressive and exclusive this event is, Gail makes it by membership only: You must present the laminated "Turkey Club" card she printed with your name on it to gain admission. She has, however, been known to invite and include others in her community who don't have a card and don't otherwise have a celebration to attend, so I think if you're in, you don't really need a card.

We meet for our Thanksgiving-in-July lunch today at The Chili Pepper, one of my favorite Mexican restaurants. My lunch with her daughter, Abby (May 25th), was the turning point for me offering any input concerning the choice of where to eat, if you will recall. I provided no input today, yet she chose a Mexican restaurant. Gail has recently begun a gluten-free food intolerance diet, and certain items on a Mexican food menu are allowed for her. Just as with any kink in life—large or small—Gail takes this inconvenience in stride. She doesn't make a big deal out of it. She rolls on, unruffled as usual.

Gail is mother to Abby (May 25th) and Kate (November 18th). She was a single mother for many years after she and their dad divorced, and then she married a former flame from college and had two more children—a son and another daughter. They are close in age to my children. This 17-year difference from her youngest to oldest is easily managed with her wide motherly wingspan.

Gail has a knack for making all things look easy, a sleight of hand, perhaps; nonetheless, she keeps so many balls in the air without dropping any from her juggling act. One of her favorite icons is Rosie the Riveter, accompanied by her famous phrase: "We Can Do It!" Gail can do whatever she sets her mind to. She has done it many times.

When Gail was on her own with her first two daughters, she managed her family *and* managed a restaurant. She kept going like a locomotive, once again tapping that rhythm when she opened a franchise donut shop when she remarried and moved to another small town in western Kansas.

It is a joke in our family that I value sleep more than almost anything else. I am known to go to bed before guests have left my home when I am the hostess. Gail compensates for her sister's shortcoming; she can survive—and frequently did—on only several hours of sleep when she was the owner and sole proprietor of the donut shop.

I think all seven of our parents' children came to their own realizations about the brevity of life after they died. Some of us made visible changes, others kept the changes inside. Eight months after Mom and Dad died, Gail closed her donut shop doors after seven years of business. She wanted to give more time back to her family; they missed her, and she missed them. She is now the office manager for a chiropractor in her town. She manages the office well; anything Gail is put in charge of runs like a well-oiled machine. She gets to sleep all night now but does choose to stay up late to celebrate small and large events—unlike her sister.

She and her family have come to visit mine this weekend to celebrate Independence Day. My husband and I host a gathering for family and friends annually on the eve of our nation's birth. Gail and I take a trip to town to dine and shop, as we frequently do when she has made the 3½- hour trip. Most of our siblings will join us for the party tomorrow. Mom and Dad always came to our gatherings, too, so we carry on in their honor, choosing to spend time together as adult siblings because we enjoy each other's company. They taught us how to be at peace with each other, and how to have our own Independence Day every day.

"We Can Do It!" We *are* doing it. Gail has stepped into her matriarch role as effortlessly as she has taken on any other management job, and she is managing us well. With Gail to look up to, we are all as strong as Rosie.

GAIL'S LUNCH DATE

If there is anyone who holds a candle to keeping friends like I do, it is likely Gail. She makes friends for life like I do, but all of us—myself included, obviously—need to reach out a little more than we do.

Gail worked with Sue for four years before she opened her donut shop. She and Sue were secretaries to Grant and Elliot, two brothers who capably ran their own insurance business. Sue and Gail were their right and left hands respectively—Gail is left-handed—and most likely, they couldn't have done it without these two amazing women.

As Gail's yearning for her own show prevailed and landed her in her donut shop, Sue was left to manage capably and wholly until Gail's replacement showed up, *not that Gail can be replaced.* Gail and Sue would see each other in passing, but, Gail said, she didn't stay close enough to Sue. They were friends, Sue and Gail, but in a small town, one naturally assumes you will see each other often enough without making an effort. They would meet in passing, but without their daily interactions, they didn't stay close. Life moved on.

Life, however, happened to both of them: Gail suffered the same loss I did, and Sue lost her good health to breast cancer. Gail knew she would reach out to Sue through her struggles, in time. The time, however, passed, and Gail hadn't yet gone to visit Sue, nor had she seen her in passing. Sue was back to work in the office, and she was surviving through treatment and recovery.

Gail's restaurant management history was at the Pizza Hut in Osborne, the town our parents lived in. From 1982 to 1995, she capably managed this iconic franchise restaurant, cranking out awesome pizzas, pasta dishes and sandwiches, and employing many people in this small town. Our sister, Suzanne (December 29th), worked for her, as did many other young people in transition. Gail was capable, driven, and pushed her employees to produce. Suzanne tells the story of the sign she posted, which embodied her philosophy of down time for her employees:

IF YOU HAVE TIME TO LEAN,
YOU HAVE TIME TO CLEAN.

Historically, Gail has wasted no time on any job-related task. She is efficient and productive, but sometimes, as my argument states from the beginning of this book, such productivity can be counter-productive when it makes one too *busy*. (Ugh, the dreaded 'b' word.) Because she is my sister, I am going to say this, this observation that I might not make about someone I wasn't related to, someone who could disown me: Gail wasted time in reaching out to Sue. She was too *busy*. So, she took this pay-it-forward opportunity to make it happen.

In this small town, the choices for carry-out food are limited. When it came time for Gail to pay her lunch date forward, she chose to pick up Pizza Hut pizza and take it to Sue at the office. She chose to do it at that moment, wasting no more time.

Gail has a gift for making and keeping friends—almost as good as I am—and keeping Sue as her friend proved to be as easy as taking a pizza to her. They renewed their friendship, and the gap was bridged. Sue remains in good health and will likely continue to keep the office well-oiled and running smoothly. Of course, it will never be the same without Gail—nothing is—but Sue will continue to capably be the right-hand(ed) Girl Friday.

Gail, on the other hand—the left hand—will keep her office running smoothly as her chiropractic boss keeps their patients running smoothly.

More importantly, Gail will continue to be the matriarch, the *Rosie* our family continues to look up to.

WE CAN DO IT!

7/13: AMY

It is fitting that I write about Amy's lunch date as the maiden voyage on my new laptop. After all, I have a history of new beginnings with her.

I met Amy on February 24th, 1990. I remember the date because it was exactly one week after   I arrived, alone and scared, in suburban Philadelphia. I signed up for a one-year adventure as a nanny for two children, ages two and four. Amy signed up to take care of three kids, and arrived on the same day, through the same agency. The agency gave us each other's names and phone numbers and made a match that has lasted more than 21 years. We arranged to meet at her new home— a rowhouse in downtown Philadelphia. I knew as soon as she opened the door that I would like her.

I was out of college almost two years and drifting like a gypsy through several jobs that didn't fill me up. My now-husband had taken a break from our brief dating relationship, and I needed to find a new life—or shall I say I needed to *get* one. I found a temporary one and stayed just two days past the one-year mark.

Amy possessed—and still exudes—a quiet energy. Her temperament is one of calm gracefulness, both physically and socially. She is that way by nature, but her long history of running enhances it. I am forever envious of her long, lithe legs, but she helped me shape up my short ones. She suggested I join her for an early morning run at the end of May in 1990, but it had been since high school for me, and, well, I just really didn't want to. I was done with running six years before that.

Amy didn't accept that as an answer. She continued to gently coax and encourage me, and I couldn't ignore her. For two weeks, I met her at 5:30 am for a run, and I was hooked. Aside from taking short respites just before and after having two babies, I have taken a morning run almost every day since.

I give credit to Amy for the strength I get from running as a large part of my saving grace since the morning after my world fell apart. I wish I could write words strong enough to express my gratitude to her for holding my hand for those two weeks in May of 1990 to get me running again, but they don't exist. Trust me, I make my living with words, and there are none. I wouldn't have survived so well without the peace I continue to feel inside from my daily run. All I can say is *thank you,* my dear friend.

We meet today in Minneapolis, Minnesota, where she lives with her husband and three children. My husband, our two sons and I are vacationing here, after two nights in Des Moines with my husband's sister, and two nights before that in Kansas City with friends. We came here for friends and fishing for my husband and older son. For my younger son, we came to the Mall of America as a long-anticipated mecca to the Lego store. For me, I get to see two of my dearest friends.

Our neighbors at home—Kelly and Mike— just moved here a month ago. You met Kelly on January 22nd. Amy moved back here after three years with her Philly family; her parents still live in her hometown an hour away. She and I both married builders, have both continued to run, and as I write this, I realize we both ended up mothering the same number of kids we took care of in our nanny days. She grew up in an Irish-Catholic family with seven siblings; I grew up with six in a German-Catholic family. More than all of those similarities, I like her because she understands me, and I like to think it is mutual.

Her girls have grown in the five years since last my visit, and I get to meet her son, Owen, for the first time. He was born three days after her 42nd birthday; he is now 2 ½. Anna is six, she waited patiently for the first year of her life in China for her adoptive parents to take her home. Like most Chinese girls adopted into other countries, Anna was carefully left in a public place with milk and diapers, but no history. The Chinese government chose to assign her my father's birthday, so I have a special fondness for her. Megan was born one month before her older sister arrived from China; Amy had planned to make the trip with her husband, but her sister became the proxy.

Amy and I had good intentions of enjoying our lunch today in one of the finer restaurants in this behemoth mall, the one and only Mall of America in Minneapolis, Minnesota, but after satisfying my son with a Subway sandwich and chips, we realized that not much had changed since our more youthful days in Philadelphia: we both enjoy shopping more than eating. We sacrificed the fine dining for fast Mexican food—it was her idea—so that we could maximize our shopping time. It was reminiscent of our many trips to the legendary malls in King of

Prussia, Pennsylvania. We shopped and bought and provided the same peer pressure we once did for each other: now we both own a new pair of shoes neither of us really needed, but *wanted*, so we indulged. (Okay, turns out she *did* need a new pair of black sandals, but I can't argue the same for myself.) And, true to form from the old days, I bought more than she did. Really, can a woman own *too many* Life is Good® shirts? I didn't think so, especially when there is an entire store right here that is devoted to their wonderful products that embody my personal philosophy.

Our time together is too short as always, and she has to leave after lunch to retrieve her children from Carmen, her friend whom I am lucky to have met in years past. It is too trite, too overused to say that it feels that no time has passed since our last visit. It has. She gained another child; I lost two people I loved fiercely. I have since become a writer and hopefully soon an author, she and her husband have added two rooms onto opposite ends of their home. Our children have grown, and we have aged five years, even though our first comment to each other after a greeting hug was, "You look just the same!" Indeed, time has passed, and it will continue to slip away faster than we wish it would. Life ebbs and flows, but our friendship has passed the test of time and life changes. Thanks to her, I will keep running, and that energy will fuel my writing, as well as everything else I choose to do in my life. She will keep running, too, and we will see each other again as soon as we can.

Somehow, way back on February 24th, 1990, I knew I had just met a lifelong friend. Perhaps now, you can see why.

AMY'S LUNCH DATE

I read that when the guy who invented the sticky note proposed his plan, he was laughed at. The consensus was that this was a crazy idea. Nobody would ever use them. They were wrong.

Amy was wrong about Julie. She met Julie when they both worked one high school summer at 3M, the home of the sticky note. Both of their fathers worked there, and they were part of a summer work program.

Amy is earthy and natural; her vibrant red hair is all the color she needs. Julie wore red on her lips—too much lipstick, in Amy's opinion.

When Amy met her during orientation, she was sure they wouldn't have anything in common; no reason to become friends.

Amy found a friend in Julie. In this unlikely pairing, Julie and Amy became closer than they thought they could be on Day One. They became fast work friends during their summer together at 3M, but those three months were soon finished, and they went their separate ways.

As life goes, and as in most reunions I wrote about for this book, they hadn't seen each other for far too long, so Julie became Amy's lunch date choice.

It had been about five years, but Julie gladly accepted Amy's invitation to lunch. She was still in the Minneapolis area but was preparing to move to sunny and warmer Florida with her husband. The timing of their lunch date was just right for a send-off to the Sunshine State, so they got to see each other one last time before she moved.

Since then, Amy reports, they have maintained loose contact, getting in touch at least once a year with Christmas cards. It's hard to say, but Amy feels that perhaps without this last lunch date, they may have lost touch with each other. Their lives are vastly different from each other's, but the 3M connection still sticks—just like the idea of the sticky note did.

7/22: CHRISTINA

"So, *you're* Kathleen Depperschmidt!" said the young, beautiful blonde barista at what is now Moka's, one of my most frequented lunch locations. This was about seven years ago— in their pre-magnetic strip gift-card days— when I approached the counter with my coffee. A friend had given me a gift certificate to Caper's Coffee Shop, and it worked like a tab: You simply give them your name when you check out, and they deduct your purchase from your balance.

I recall responding with a dazed, "Who *are* you?" I'm sure I made a fabulous first impression.

I know my name attracts attention; I am used to that. So, when Christina was given my name as the therapist she would be observing at the hospital, it stuck in her mind. She was finishing her undergraduate degree in Spanish at a small local college. Because there were no classes allowing her to receive college credit for observation in the professional field she aspired to, they simply created one for her. *That's* how special she is. She completed the necessary observation hours the following semester and returned several years later after I left the hospital to complete her hands-on training as an intern. She went on to receive her master's degree in speech-language pathology and is now employed by that same hospital. I have watched her perform near-miracles with all ages in our field, but she currently works with the birth-to-three-year-old population. She also covers for me in my work with adults, because she has the time, and she says she needs the money. Perhaps she does; she is getting married two weeks and one day from today. On August 5th, she will become Mrs. Christina Nelson, marrying the man who's been the love of her life for the past seven years. She is only 25, but wise beyond that quarter century. I'm pretty sure there is an old soul in there.

Because, after lunch date number 26, I vowed to offer no persuasion whatsoever as to our dining choice, I left it completely up to her. As with all decisions large and small, she made a good one. We drove through the carryout window at Gourmet To Go, a restaurant just down the hill from my office. They serve several choices daily, and as their name would suggest, it is available only to go. I had yet to enjoy their fare, and I am thankful to her for introducing me to what will likely become a stop that is far too convenient and tasty for me to by-pass on the way to my office.

We drove away and, as with so many other dates, we drove on to my office. This time we actually dined there. She hadn't seen it since I put on the finishing touches. Thanks to my dear friend, Kelly (my lunch date exactly six months ago today on January 22nd), my space there is so cozy, and the décor simply flows. She can take any interior and bring it to life. (She came up in last week's lunch date story, so is it obvious how much I miss her?)

Christina and I enjoy our Greek pita sandwiches, and the tasty dressing drips down my chin. I can't help it, I am a passionate eater, and sometimes it shows too much. That doesn't matter with Christina, because I can let it all hang out with her, and I usually do. She knows me well, and she has kept me in spite of this. She is young and energetic; I joke that I am old and jaded, but it isn't always a joke. I have offered her whatever measures of professional knowledge I can share, but more important than that, I have tried to show her "the ropes" of our profession. Today, she thanks me for that, as she frequently does. Sometimes those ropes bind, and sometimes they burn, but they are part of the package deal we have all signed up for as speech therapists. The professional knowledge I have shared with her has now been eclipsed by her prodigious insight and intellect, as well as her varied work experiences. She shines like a million-watt light bulb, and I can only hope she will remember me when her name is famous in our professional circles.

She's not striving for fame or fortune; she is simply following her heart. She is a good listener in conversation, and she has a finely-tuned ear for listening to that little voice inside—the one that is an intuitive blend of heart and mind. This voice is telling her to pursue her passions with a specialized early childhood speech therapy program she has trained extensively for. It is also telling her to *go west young woman*, as in *Colorado*. I am so happy for her, because now I can live vicariously there through her *and* Christie (March 3rd), as she is making plans to move there too. Christina completed her internship at the hospital with Christy as her supervisor, and as a natural result of spending extensive amounts of time with her, she has remained close to Christy as well.

(Christy is like flypaper: you just can't get away from her, and you don't really want to.)

Now, all this is great for them, and it will be for me when I visit there, but until I get my place there (I think my lottery numbers are going to match up *soon*), I will be just a tiny bit jealous. You see, Colorado beckons me to stay every time I go there with my sisters (see September 3rd). The Rocky Mountain High is too intoxicating for me to forget, and I will make it my second home *someday*. Until then, I may overstay my welcome with both of them.

I am old enough to be Christina's mother, but this generation between us seems to be only a tiny gap, not an abyss. There are several women in the generation before me in this book (Jane Ann—December 1st, Dot—December 6th, Lois—October 3rd, Ila—March 12th) whom I consider my friends, yet I look up to them. I can only hope Christina feels a fraction of this esteem for me. I hope I deserve it.

CHRISTINA'S LUNCH DATE—as written by Christina

I don't believe in coincidences. I guess I don't have to. I know that God has a plan for my life. I have been blessed to never have had doubts about this, but this has never been more evident than in the past year. The fact that I was one of the "chosen" ones who had the opportunity to have a lunch date with Kathleen wasn't a coincidence. The fact that my best friend recently lost her son in a battle with cancer wasn't a coincidence either. My friends don't believe in coincidences, either.

The fact that my internship supervisor would have a pre-paid tab at the coffee shop I worked at and that she would have such a memorable name (you can't forget Depperschmidt!) wasn't a coincidence. Since that time eight years ago, I have become one of the lucky people in this world who Kathleen considers a friend. This is not something to take for granted. Being a friend of Kathleen's means that she will always remember your birthday and the little details that others will forget about you. Most of all, this means she will be your friend for life. She will make every effort to keep in touch with you and make an impact on your life. This book and the idea for this book is a perfect example of this.

When I grow up, I want to be like Kathleen. When I first met Kathleen in Caper's coffee shop (now Moka's) I wanted to be like her because she was a speech-language pathologist, the career I was working so hard to eventually have. It didn't take long for me to realize I want to be like Kathleen for many more reasons. I want to be like Kathleen because she is an amazing friend. Kathleen is just downright cool. She is stylish and fun. She is smart and successful (despite telling me at my first day of my internship that there is no reason to be an overachiever). I want to be like Kathleen because she knows when to break the rules.

After I had my lunch date with Kathleen, I tried to think of which friend I really needed to connect with. I wanted to be like Kathleen— that amazing friend who always keeps in touch. But the more I tried to do what she asked, the more I realized that I couldn't follow the rules. I knew that part of wanting to be like Kathleen when I grow up means that I am allowed to break rules. I already had a weekly (sometimes bi-weekly or even tri-weekly) lunch date. I wasn't making the effort to find someone I needed to connect with and describe our detailed lunch date. However, if this lunch date book was the "coincidence" that allowed me to share the story of multiple lunch dates, I had to break the rules.

My friend, Allison, and I became friends at work. I am a pediatric speech-language pathologist; she is a pediatric physical therapist—the best I have ever seen. She isn't the best I have ever seen because she knows every bit of research available or because she has extensive experience working with children with various disabilities (although she does have these skills). She is the best I have ever seen because she cares. She wants to make a difference in the lives of the children and families she works with. Since we had the opportunity to work together, we were able to spend lunch together frequently. Our passion for our clients brought us together; our lunch dates together over the past year tied us together for life.

I started working with and going on lunch dates with Allison when she was pregnant. Little did I know that this baby was going to make me a better person, friend and Christian. We weren't friends for long when I got the phone call early one October Tuesday morning— "Christina, I am so scared, Reed has a lump on his stomach." I told my friend, Allison, that there is no reason to worry. This was probably nothing; this couldn't possibly be cancer or something serious. Those are things that happen to people you don't know. Wow, was I wrong.

I am amazed at how those months seem so clear and like such a blur at the same time. The diagnosis, the days/weeks/months of constantly changing answers, the sadness, the waiting, the trips to Children's Mercy hospital, the bruises, the lost hair, the overwhelming support from the community, the smiles from a little boy, the hope, the constant reminder that God is love. The way that, despite going through the most difficult pain imaginable, my best friend and her husband developed stronger faith. The devastatingly sad March day that Reed passed away.

My way of being there for Allison was by being there for her in little ways. I wish I could take credit for the ways that I was there for her. I prayed for months that I would be a vessel for the Lord to show her his love. I watched my mentor, Kathleen; I learned from her about how to be there for a grieving friend. When everyone else moved on, I wanted to continue to be there for Allison. I wanted to think and talk about Reed because I knew that she will never want to stop thinking and talking about him.

Our lunch dates turned into a set Monday schedule of chicken and noodles at Jim's Chicken, a small local fried chicken place in Salina, Kansas. It seemed nice to have consistency to comfort us in an unpredictable world. Every Monday, we had a date. Every Monday we had the same meal—homemade chicken noodles on top of mashed potatoes with a salad from the salad bar. Some days we were quiet, some days we laughed, other days we cried. When you go through what we went through together, you don't always have to talk. For her, I knew that some days were difficult—and those were the easy ones. I wish I could tell you how much I needed those lunch dates and Allison's constant friendship. She knew about the stresses I was undergoing as a bride-to-be/newlywed dealing with my parents' divorce, my grandmother's illness, my sister's recent miscarriage and the hardships of being an official "grown-up."

It is not a coincidence that despite having many Monday lunch dates, there is one that sticks out to me more than any other. It was a Monday in February. After several days of not seeing my friend as she tended to her sick child, I had the opportunity to have lunch with her on a Monday at Jim's Chicken for chicken noodles. Our lunch date required a larger table in the back because we were accompanied by our thoughtful friend, Jana, Allison's husband Josh, and a little boy who wanted to be held by his mom and dad through the entire meal. He hadn't eaten solids in many days, and before that he had only eaten

Reese's peanut butter cups (I think this may have something to do with his older brother's name being Reese). Despite his body not allowing him to seem like the same little boy he was a few months prior, I remember how he looked at his parents with loving eyes. I remember not knowing what to say but knowing that that was okay. I remember a conversation filled with tears and fears as Josh and Allison began contemplating experimental measures to give them more time with their son. I remember the hope in Josh and Allison's eyes as he took bites of homemade coleslaw and mashed potatoes. I remember a day when Josh and Allison cherished their little boy, and he cherished his parents.

It is not a coincidence that despite my recent move to Colorado that I am (and always will be) close to Allison and Kathleen. It is not a coincidence that Kathleen was my friend and I learned how to be a better friend to others, especially those who are grieving. It is not a coincidence that I worked with Allison or became friends with her right before the most difficult time in her life. It is not a coincidence that Reed was a part of our lives. It is not a coincidence that there is a little one on the way for Josh and Allison. It is not a coincidence that God is good and so are my friends. It is not a coincidence that this book ended up in your hands.

7/26: DARCEE

I have a beautiful, zippered cardigan sweater that is rich with fall colors. I bought it about 16 years ago, and it is probably the oldest article of clothing I still wear regularly. Okay, so I wear it exactly once a year, and once a year only. It is in my possession for only half of the year, and I have to fit it in among the ridiculous number of other sweaters waiting their turn.

For the remainder of the year, it sits in my friend, Darcee's, closet—except for the one day a year she wears it. You see, it is a bit worn and outdated, yet we each make a point to wear it once a year.

I found it on the clearance rack, and I couldn't resist it. I wore it to work, and Darcee saw it.

"*You* bought that sweater!" she said to me when I ran into her. "I saw it and wanted it, but I didn't get it. It was the last one at Maurice's, wasn't it?" Indeed, it was.

I felt guilty for "stealing" it away from her; I could tell she loved it. It quickly became obvious to me what I had to do: it didn't really belong just to me, I had to share it with her. And so began a long tradition of exchanging the sweater twice a year to allow each of us at least one wearing. It is old and outdated, but it still garners compliments.

Darcee and I meet at Wood Fashion Café, where I dined with Shelly on April 1st, and my husband on April 22nd. She enters with a big gift bag. Simply exchanging the sweater isn't enough for each of us. In the bag, we take turns adding a gift, usually something to adorn the other's home. She is lucky to live in her dream home just like me, so we like to help each other add to the beauty.

I met Darcee in 1994, shortly after I began my speech therapy career. I started as a school-based therapist, and she is part of the therapy trinity within the schools: She is an occupational therapist, just like Nancy whom you met on February 7th. She works with children's fine motor and perceptual deficits. (The third member to complete the therapy trio is the physical therapist.) I knew I wanted to keep her, and she let me. I would leave our mutual workplace after four years, but she continues to make a difference in the lives of the school-age children. She has *that* gift, among her many others.

Darcee and her husband live outside our small city in the opposite direction, not far from Stacy (August 22nd). They have no children, but she knows the importance of family. She is close to her parents and her sister, who, coincidentally (I really don't believe *anything* is a coincidence), lived close to me in the dormitory during my freshman year of college. Her sister has recently battled and won the fight with breast cancer, and Darcee soldiered on with her from diagnosis to the last treatment.

My parents' funeral packed the large church to capacity, and I will be forever grateful to each and every one of the people who came to pay their respects and offer support. There were many friends of each of their seven children there, with only very few of them never having met my parents. Darcee was one of those few. She didn't know them, but understood the funeral wasn't just for the deceased. More importantly, it is for the living loved ones left behind. She traveled 100 miles to be there for me, and I will never forget that. She's never walked this path, but yet she understands. I'm pretty sure her heart is pure gold.

Darcee hasn't experienced tragedy; I hope she never does. Yet, she has an awareness, a sense of insight and empathy when other's lives shatter. She knows to come right away and help pick up the pieces, even if she doesn't have a clue where to put them after she picks them up. She just does it, and she does it with a true sense of caring. Perhaps it is her job, as she works with other people's hands all day. She just possesses that gift of knowing what a hurting person needs.

That sweater beckoned me from the cedar chest the other day. I saw it there, knowing it needed its due for the fall. I need to wear it at least once, and get it to Darcee, along with a gift. She doesn't need anything, but one never *needs* gifts. Much like friends, we *want* them.

I am recalling the thoughtfulness Darcee showed me when my second son was born. It was a gift card to a local store, with a note that read: "Spend this on a *want*, not a *need.*" Just like in a time of unparalleled grief, she knows what a person experiencing such joy needs.

I found the perfect gift with that card. It was a small, decorative pillow with the face of the sun, and the title of the song that I would sing to my boys many times over, until they begged me to stop: *"You Are My Sunshine."*

May the sun keep shining on my friend, Darcee, and if it ever doesn't, I hope I can offer a small measure of the peace and joy she naturally brings with her to a friendship.

May both our lives remain as colorful as the fall sweater we share.

DARCEE'S LUNCH DATE

As if one talented, brilliant, highly qualified, and experienced occupational therapist (OT) in one's repertoire of friends isn't already a bonus—OTs are hard to come by—how about two? And, to further sweeten that deal, how about if they are both from the same small town in western Kansas? The same small town I sometimes drive through on my way to see my sister Gail, the same small town my stepson spent many of his formative years living in with his mother. So cool.

Andrea is an OT as well, working in the nursing home circuit I used to work in before I took the plunge into independence. I will never forget the day I met her. I had heard we were being blessed with another OT, because we needed one badly to complete our therapy trifecta. She came through the door, and her energetic aura immediately captured me. I sensed her take-charge, no holds barred, tell-it-like-it-is style, and I liked it. I still do.

Darcee has always liked that about her, as well as a myriad of large and small aspects of her personality that she has known about her for so many years, growing up together in *Hoxie, Kansas.* They both live outside of our small city now; Andrea lives about 20 minutes west of Darcee, 40 minutes from my house, forming a wide triangle. I could say this distance keeps us from meeting often enough, but, *come on.* We are all in our small city nearly every day, but we are just *too busy.* (Ugh, that word again.)

Darcee, knowing she needed to connect again with her dear friend, made a lunch date with Andrea. It had been too long. I wasn't there, but I am sure the time since their last visit fell away, and they picked right up from the last visit. I don't know the details, I don't know where they went, because I didn't persist in following up to get the story. The important thing is that they had a date, they connected just like I asked them to.

I asked permission of both of them to allow me to fill in with whatever I saw fit, because here's the deal: Andrea is my friend too, and I have always felt a bit sad inside because I didn't take her out myself. At the outset, my goal was to reach out to those people I had not seen for months if not years, and I was privileged to spend some of my recent working hours in Andrea's company. So, I did not ask her to lunch, and I know she understands. Still, I feel bad. There are a handful like her, and I am trying to make my rounds before I wrap this up.

Today is a *Snow Day* for Darcee, and for my sons as well. The weather didn't deliver the punch in the form of more ice on the Monday after the Thanksgiving weekend—we were already socked in all weekend because of the first round—but the powers that be in our local schools saw it fit to call school off last night. So, to add that to the birthday celebration for our dear friend, Dot (December 6th), we have lunch at *Olive Garden*. Dot shares her birthday with Veterans Day, and she wanted to go out later in the month, and she chose today. Darcee, Andrea and I meet her here for a late birthday lunch. Dot, if you will recall, is an Occupational Therapy assistant, so she is the Girl Friday to OTs like Darcee and Andrea. They all work with the human hand as well as the arm, in order to perform *Activities of Daily Living*—more commonly known as ADLs in therapy lingo. These activities include dressing, grooming, cooking, writing and all those other abilities most of us take for granted.

They work with their hands to help others with their hands and arms and all the activities that entails, but mostly they work from their hearts. These three, in my estimation, are the best you will find around. Anyone can work with their hands, but it takes people like Darcee, Andrea and Dot to put their hearts into it.

Andrea knows the pain of losing her mother, and since our date, Darcee, unfortunately, now knows the pain of losing her father. I wish neither of them knew the pain of losing even one parent, but they do, and they continue to move forward in their lives. I only hope I can be of some small comfort to both of them as the months and then years of loss linger on.

Both Darcee and Andrea knew Gina; Darcee worked with her in the past. They know she was an incredible woman; anyone who knew her even a little bit knew this. Gina worked from her heart, too, making a living and a life as an OT just like Darcee and Andrea.

She is still working on my heart, telling me to keep going with this crazy project. After all, it is dedicated to her. I know she doesn't want the attention posthumously; she didn't even want it when she was here.

She simply wants me to get these stories out, she wants the world to know about all these amazing people in my life.

Perhaps she wants them to know just how special OTs really are.

EPILOGUE

As I wrap this up, a timely piece of news must be shared. Tomorrow will be Andrea's last day with our previous mutual employer: 13 lucky years are coming to an end with this company for her, just as they came to an end for me five years ago. It is time for her to move on to greener professional pastures, to a job that will liberate her from some old chains she is no longer willing to drag around. Of course, she will continue to perform her work from the heart, just in a different capacity. Darcee and I celebrated with her at lunch when she broke the good news, and tomorrow, Friday evening, we will celebrate with her after work for dinner and drinks.

At our lunch, Darcee brought me a gift—even though I didn't bring her the sweater (yet—I will tomorrow). Knowing how much I love Rosie the Riveter, she found me a shopping bag emblazoned with this iconic, strong and liberated woman.

In keeping with this appropriate theme, I found a "toast to your future" gift for Andrea. It's a water bottle with Rosie's strong arm and *WE CAN DO IT* to remind us that we are, indeed, doing it, and will continue to do it—Gail style (July 2nd). When I was wrapping it, I noticed it was made by a company so fitting for this occasion and printed in large letters across the lid: *LIBERTY*.

8/8: MICHELLE

I am sticking with my resolve *not* to sway my lunch date into choosing a restaurant I like. Today, Michelle had her choices narrowed down to three, and I offered absolutely no input. She was torn between Coco Bolos, where I dined with Shari on May 7th, Olive Garden, where I dined with Ila Martin on March 12th in Topeka, and a place I'd never heard of called *Ingredient*. Without any input from me, she chose *Ingredient*.

It was perfect. Not only was the food good, but their policy on tipping was even better: they don't accept any. Instead, the menu suggests that if you feel the need to give, you should donate money to charity, fill someone else's parking meter, pet a dog, say 'hello' to a stranger, perform a random act of kindness, or do something nice for yourself. *Pay it forward.* Perfect.

Manhattan, Kansas, is Michelle's home. She lives here with her two boys and her professor husband. It is also the home of Kansas State University. Her husband works there, which is how she knew that the wife of the president of the university sat down at the table next to us. If I'd known it was her, I would have picked up her tab, too, because if team loyalty is any indication, her husband will be in charge of my oldest son in four years.

We sat by the window, enjoying the clear skies prevailing after the morning rain. We spoke of our boys, of course, as we always do to initiate our conversations. We have more in common than just the Boys Club: we are both speech therapists, we are both runners, and we both married men named Mark.

We met in graduate school in 1992. She quickly recognized my future married name, because her parents are friends with my husband's aunt and uncle by the same (unforgettable) name. We recognized each other as runners, too, so we had a lot to talk about. We easily became friends and have remained close.

Like most of my runner friends, we compare notes on our performance on foot. She is the leader of the local Parkinson's Support Group and has organized a fun run for its benefit. I may try to get up early enough on that day in several weeks to join the fun and support her *very* worthwhile cause. She has worked in the geriatric field, and we both know the devastation that Parkinson's disease can bring. She now works part-time as a school-based therapist but continues to work as a consultant in the local nursing home circuit.

We discuss our old and new running habits; she has more drive to run in competitive races than I do. I'll chalk it up in small part to the (slight) difference in our ages; I am not as race oriented as I once was. I prefer to race against myself. She races against herself, too, but acknowledges that she still maintains a competitive spirit. I wish sometimes I had more of that, but I am happy to run slow and steady, just like the fabled tortoise. I want to be running when I am 90 years old, so I tend to take it easy, perhaps *too* easy. I know what works for me, and I counsel her that perhaps her spirit of competition keeps her from enjoying running for what it can provide her at its best: a sense of well-being. If no one could see her race times, would she still push herself so hard? She ponders that, and I glance out the window again to remind me that when you point a finger, as my mother used to say, there are three pointing back at you.

Outside our window, I see the car I drove here today. It is not my car; mine is in the shop. I have long salivated over the Dodge Charger, imagining myself cruising in this handsome ride. It is part of my pseudo-midlife crisis, I tell the saleswoman, and she lets me take a white one for the day while they fix my car. Would I still like to drive this car if no one saw me in it? I have to acknowledge these three fingers pointing back at me, and say "no." Without a doubt, it is a cool car and a powerful machine, but I was smitten only with the looks. It didn't feel right for me, and *my* sense of well-being wouldn't benefit in any wholesome way. I gladly trade it back for my car at the end of the day. Lesson learned.

Michelle's boys are with her parents for the next three days, and I encourage her to make the most of the time alone with her husband. I know too well there is so little of it when there are two young boys in the picture. We lament the fact that boys always seem to know how to push their mother's buttons to get a reaction, but seldom, if at all, do they do this to their dad. This, I have come to realize as a member of the Boys Club, is almost universal. We do also acknowledge the notion that, "If Momma ain't happy…" Well, you know the rest.

She and her husband are privileged to have adopted two children who found their way to their hearts and their home. Trewman will soon be six and came from the Midwest. Trey is eight and came from Korea. They were destined to be part of this family; I am sure of this with every adopted child I know—and I have many friends who have adopted.

While their boys are gone tonight, Michelle and her husband have a date at home to watch this book's namesake movie: *Pay It Forward*. She has yet to see it, and I have asked my dates to do their best to watch it if they already haven't. This restaurant's policy on no tips is the perfect embodiment of this theory.

We prepare to part ways; our time is too short. We have mulled over minor and major life issues, and I tell her what I tell so many people: When it comes to running, listen to your body. When it comes to decisions, listen to your little voice. The older we get, the smarter it gets. When you point a finger, focus on the three pointing back at you. I am staring at my three, and I have to leave now because the Charger is due back soon. I will be so happy once again to cruise down the road in my old, high-mileage average-Jane car. Momma is happy.

MICHELLE'S LUNCH DATE

After many failed attempts to meet with Michelle to get her story, after the sluggish delay that encompassed several years (ugh), we finally got together again specifically to get her story down. We had met many other times in between then and now, but we never took the time to talk about this. It has been so long, actually, that my son is now part of Kansas State University as a freshman. And—ironically—we met tonight at Coco Bolo's to finally finish her story. AND—wait, I will save that one for the end.

Time passes and life brings many surprises, many of them good ones. I have been invited to Kansas State University this evening to speak to a graduate-level class in speech language pathology. In this four-year period, Michelle accepted a position at KSU, and then had to leave it when it was cut due to changes in the university funding. This closed door led her to an expanded opportunity to be the regional Parkinson's Disease guru for communication and to provide general information and support—as well as therapy for patients, families and caregivers. She was a clinical supervisor for the speech-language pathology department, which gave her the opportunity to plug my first book, *The Tip of Your Tongue: A Speech Therapist's Tribute to the Power of Communication Lost and Found*. The clinical director accepted it from her, and subsequently invited me to speak to her students. *I am so grateful.* This is a golden opportunity, and I have Michelle to thank.

So back to the lunch date. I anticipated that all my lunch dates would report back to me with flowery, happily ended stories of how they reconnected with someone they needed to spend more time with. I expected that I would help them fill at least a small hole inside that was vacated by a friendship/relationship that needed to be tended to. I thought everyone would live happily ever after.

Michelle set out to do just that. She had an acquaintance that she felt could become a friend because of the mutual activities their children engaged in, and they didn't live far from each other. She felt that Beth likely felt the same way, so she asked her to lunch. I don't know a soul who doesn't feel drawn to Michelle's charm and wide smile when they meet her, her boundless energy toward all things bright and good.

Sometimes, even as a middle-aged woman, I realize, I am still naïve.

Beth didn't reciprocate. She didn't give Michelle the return she'd hoped for. She remained mostly distant during their lunch, and that was that.

Sometimes, life is just so hard. We think we know how to read someone, and then something like this slaps us in the face. We think we got the green light to reach out, and our hand gets slapped.

I do know I am not quite as naïve as I once was about one thing: we can never know what another person is facing inside. I have learned this the hard way. Michelle did go on to learn from events that took place not long after that Beth had her own set of struggles. Some of Beth's actions made sense when Michelle put the pieces together, but a few remained a mystery. Some stung Michelle a bit, because, like me, her heart is out on her sleeve sometimes.

"We are all sensitive people, with so much to give." The lyrics from the random song on my Pandora station just spoke that to me at the very moment I wrote the previous line. So true, and so timely.

**

Back to that other thing I almost told you earlier: I didn't buy the Charger, and I am still driving Scarlett, the VW I purchased just before my October 3rd dinner date with Lois—be sure to read the story. Our other car, the long-loved family truckster—the Chrysler Pacifica—finally laid down to eternal rest about six months ago, so we replaced it with a Subaru Outback. We purchased it the same day we took our son to his first day at KSU. It is a beautiful, rich gray. It is the same car—and the same color—as Michelle's Subaru.

With their boys, their work opportunities, their lives as liberated women AND as owners of their cars, these mommas are happy.

8/17: RHONDA

It is hard to get a lunch date with Rhonda. She works full-time, and she has a lunch date nearly *every day*. She goes to her mother's apartment to fix her lunch and dines with her. Almost *every day*. Rhonda and her sister take good care of their mother; she is a lucky woman.

Today, however, I am the lucky woman. I am privileged to treat Rhonda to lunch on her 50th birthday. She has chosen Hong Kong Buffet, the local Chinese smorgasbord. She has been granted a little extra time off work to dine today; she works as a histology technologist—aka, "histo-tech"—at a local laboratory. She prepares human tissue and lab samples to be examined by a doctor.

I met Rhonda through a garage sale. Not *at* a garage sale, but as a result of my neighbor's garage sale. Winona—"Nonie"—is Rhonda's mother-in-law, and she lives across the highway from me. About ten years ago, I wandered over to her big event, and I acquired the first of many second-hand, first-rate, *very* stylish articles of clothing. Oh, and they fit me *perfectly*.

Now, Nonie is a fashionable woman, but something told me these weren't her clothes.

"No, these aren't mine," she said. "They belong to my daughter-in-law, Rhonda; she lives just a few miles away on Buffalo Road." I knew where Buffalo Road was, but I didn't yet know Rhonda. Now I do, and I regret that we lived this close and didn't meet sooner—and not because I was already missing out on a lot of cool cast-offs. I'm thankful we made the connection.

As I write this several weeks after our lunch, I am recalling conversations Rhonda and I have had about our friendship. She tells me she had given up on finding good friends in this rural area, it hadn't worked out yet with anyone else, and it was too much work to keep trying. Now, more than ten years after that garage sale, we relish the connection, as well as the other friends we have made in our area since then. We all live north of our small city, and I have fondly dubbed our group

"The North Stars." Almost every morning, she runs and/or walks with Shelly (April 1st), and until Kelly (January 22nd) moved away, she exercised with her, too. As I mentioned previously in Amy's (July 13th) story, my running is slow and steady, and I am still fast asleep when they take off in the wee hours of the morning. Plus, I haven't had my caffeine fix yet, so I let them knock themselves out early in the morning. I'm happy with my slow pace, and I don't want to hold them back.

Occasionally, however, I do run with Rhonda. Her legs are a bit shorter than mine, but much faster. I have to hustle to keep up. I enjoy these infrequent runs but, better than that, I savor her company after the run while we savor good coffee.

Even better than all these attributes—cool clothes, fellow runner, I adore Rhonda for the no-nonsense friend she is. I am blessed to have so many friends, but there are times when women's sensitive feelings cause small cracks that can linger over time and require repair. Rhonda's heart is pure gold, but she doesn't let emotions cloud her judgment. I wish I could turn mine off to be as tough as her when the need arises, but I fear I am sentenced to life with my heart on my sleeve. Rhonda speaks her mind without hurting anyone else's feelings and moves on. Life is too short for her to let such trivialities bring her down. It is white, or it is black, and she makes this clear from the start. Like she shares her clothes, I wish she could share some of that with me. It's not that easy, but she inspires me to let the small, petty issues remain in the past and move forward.

Rhonda is mother to two grown girls, and grandmother to two children. Her daughters are strong and resilient like her and have made good lives for themselves through hard work just as their mother taught them through example. Rhonda was a single mother for many years during their earlier years and had no choice but to press on and make it work *somehow*. She was given some reprieve when she married Nonie's son but hasn't lost her drive to work hard.

She has, however, allowed herself to play hard, too. She travels to the Rocky Mountains in Colorado several times a year to visit her youngest daughter, who works at a ski resort. This is a sweet deal for Rhonda because she loves to ski. She earns her time off, and she uses it well.

She visits her older daughter frequently as well. She will soon graduate as a nurse practitioner after many years of study. This feat wouldn't have been possible without Rhonda's help and dedication because her daughter gave birth to the first of Rhonda's two grandchildren at age 15. She was there to see her through it all.

She laments that she sometimes spends too much money on clothes, but I'm not complaining because her spirit of giving has filled my closet nicely over the years. She gives freely of her time, money, and energy, not just her clothes. She volunteers at the local animal shelter, taking the dogs running with her when she can. She gives her time to a friend with a child with special needs, but nobody scores higher than her mother. I am keenly aware of the uncertainty of guaranteed time that anybody of any age has, especially my age group with their parents. Her father died suddenly when he was 39, so she knows this all too well, and she doesn't let a day go by without seeing her mother.

We wrap up our lunch, because, even though it is her big day, she does have to get back to work. We open our fortune cookies. Hers is a bust, and mine doesn't seem to make much sense for me, either: *"Don't worry about the stock market, your investment is good."*

While I do have a stock market account, I pay a trusted advisor to manage it for me because I don't understand it. I've made a good investment with Rhonda, I understand her well, and I don't worry a bit: I know this investment will continue to grow in value.

RHONDA'S LUNCH DATE

It is hard to describe Rhonda in such a short story. There are so many aspects of Rhonda that, as a friend for several years now, I continue to discover. I gave her credit for moving past small things and letting the past be the past, because she does. She did, however, need a little prompting to decide upon her lunch date. There were many others who did also, but it is important to the rest of this story that I tell you what I said to prompt her.

She couldn't decide who to fulfill her pay-it-forward obligation with. She mentioned this several times, and I told her this several times: *Who is the person that, if you saw their name in the obituaries tomorrow, you would never forgive yourself for not reaching out to them?* Each time I suggested this guideline, I could see the wheels turning in her head, but *I had no idea....*

I told you in her lunch date story that Rhonda had given up on making new friends. I also told you that she moves past small things. I didn't know there was one thing she never moved past that has kept her from making new friends for far too many years. She decided it was time to move past *that one thing* and put the past behind her.

This is where my book gets complicated.

I tried to leave my parents in the introduction, assigning them a large, well-deserved, but passive role in this project. I wanted you to know that their inspiration moved me to decide upon this undertaking. I wanted to pay them homage in the lunch date stories where their lives and deaths were part of my reaching out to those who were grieving. I wanted you to know how they played a role in many of my subjects' lives. Past that, I wanted to take it from there myself, because they had given me the strength.

It wasn't meant to be that way.

My mother had a letter prepared to be read at her funeral to her children. In it, she first made sure we knew how much she loved us and left us with other words that will forever keep our hearts warm. Then, promising us it would be the last time she would try to tell us what to do, she asked us to live our lives by the Prayer of St. Francis. If you are not familiar with it, look it up, and know this: it leaves no room for anything but making or keeping peace.

It is a challenge I try to live out every day, but sometimes I fail miserably. Most of my friends know about this challenge, and many were among the 500 people present at my parents' funeral. They know I try. Maybe they even get tired of me trying and failing, but they haven't lost faith in me yet. I don't think my mom—or my dad— has yet, either. My father's middle name was Francis. He is in on this, too.

Here's what I think: I think they helped Rhonda with this one. More than any other subject in this book, she exemplified the role of peacemaker. She put forth a Herculean effort, working through her fear, regret and bad memories in order to make peace with someone from long ago.

Tamie and Rhonda were best friends in high school, but it had been 35 years since they called themselves friends, and instead became enemies. All because of—you guessed it—a guy.

After a complex cascade of misunderstandings, they parted ways in bitter fashion. They were both 16. They didn't speak for the last two years of high school, and in the future when they would cross paths in our small city—they both remained in this town—they might or might not make eye contact, and their best moments were a forced "hello" from one or the other. Their 25-year class reunion was uncomfortable, with forced civilities between them for the sake of the rest of the class.

The pain didn't go away for either of them. Rhonda told me she found out during their lunch date that Tamie came to the hospital to see Rhonda's first daughter after she was born; the local grapevine informed her of the birth. She didn't stop to see Rhonda: she was too scared. She peeked into the nursery at the beautiful baby girl named *Tisha Lynn. Lynn* is Tamie's middle name. Rhonda gave her that name in honor of Tamie. Tamie didn't know that.

Rhonda did the brave, smart, hard, heroic thing: she contacted Tamie via a handwritten letter and asked her to be her lunch date to fulfill this mission. In this letter, she told Tamie about her friend, Kathleen, whose parents died, how she was writing this book, and she wanted to reach out to the important people in her life. Kathleen wanted them to do the same. Rhonda told Tamie, after all this time and all this bitterness, that she wanted to reach out to her, and try to put it behind them. Would she agree to a lunch date?

Tamie responded quickly with a return letter, and they made a plan to meet the following Saturday. Their lunch date took place at—where else—Moka's. They met at noon. The staff at Moka's gently ushered them out at closing time: 5:00 p.m.

In those five hours, they made peace. I'm pretty sure my parents were there, too.

They both spoke of the pain they carried around for 35 years, the regret surrounding the lost time. They both felt the weight of this loss and spoke of how it held them down.

When she was telling me about her lunch date, Rhonda did something she rarely does: she opened up and told me about her feelings. She told me she had great difficulty making friends since then because it hurt too much after the loss of Tamie's friendship. She told me it was too hard to reach out when she was still carrying all that weight from her failed friendship with Tamie. It was easier to *not* reach out and *not* try to make new friends. The fear and regret ruled all those years of her young life. So, she didn't reach out.

I was lucky. Our friendship didn't involve Rhonda reaching out, it just happened. It was smooth and easy. It was meant to be that Nonie would have that garage sale with all those cool clothes of Rhonda's. It was meant that they would fit me so well, just like Rhonda's friendship fits nicely into my life.

Rhonda and Tamie didn't expect to pick up where they left off. Thirty-five years of bitterness did fall away, but their lives have changed, and they both realize and respect that. They are simply taking it one day at a time. If their friendship blossoms again, they will both be happy with that. If not, they will both be at peace with their mutual pasts, and their lives will be lighter without all that weight.

"Make me an instrument of your peace," the Prayer of St. Francis begins. I didn't do the work on this peacemaking venture. I was simply an instrument...a catalyst. Still, I feel my mother—and my father, too—smiling down upon me for starting this ball rolling. They are smiling upon Rhonda and Tamie, too, I just know it.

8/22: STACY

When I was in high school, there was a girl in another high school not quite an hour from mine named Stacy. She was cute and funny, and she seemed nice, too. However, all the guys in my small high school noticed her. Consequently, none of the *girls* in my high school liked her. I didn't know her then; I didn't let it bother me too much.

Today I am having lunch with Stacy. She is still cute and funny, and even nicer than I ever knew her to be in high school. We live just outside our small city in opposite directions: she lives eight miles south; I live six miles north. Our husbands became friends through a mutual friend, and by virtue of their friendship, Stacy became my friend. Her demeanor and welcoming style made it easy.

We meet today on her end of town at Applebee's, a classic favorite. As always, the food is tasty and plentiful. However, she tells me she doesn't like to go out to lunch. In this case, she made a special exception. She is a hairdresser, operating out of a shop in her home. In order to have a lunch date, she has to create space in the middle of her workday and drive into town. It is much easier for her *not* to go out for lunch. She tells me I am worth the interruption. I am so honored. I scored two hard-to-get lunch dates two weeks in a row. I'm feeling pretty lucky right now.

Today *is* my lucky day, because 22 is my lucky number. Coincidentally, Stacy's lucky number is exactly half of mine, 11. It has been her lucky number since she was a teenager, and there have been many uncanny coincidences between her and that number. In about three months, Stacy and I—and whoever else joins us—will celebrate a once-in-forever event: 11-11-11. On November 11th of this year, these numbers will line up on the calendar just perfectly for her, and she won't let it pass without fanfare. She's not sure yet what will take place, but it will be unlike any other day and night of her life.

I have a daily calendar with tear-off pages by the famous artist, Mary Engelbreit. She pairs her artwork with a short phrase that serves as a life lesson. This calendar was my mother's favorite, and in honor of her, I buy a new one each year and give the pages away to the people I think should have them. My mom did that, too. Stacy understands: her mother is in heaven with mine. Today's page shows a young girl laughing, with these wise words: "She who laughs, lasts." On this 22nd day of the month—this number that is double her lucky number—she accepts this token with her own hearty laugh.

Stacy is the mother of two grown children—one girl, one boy. Her daughter has two small boys, ages three and five. She is the epitome of a doting grandmother. I can see her face light up at the mention of their names. Not yet near that point in my life, I can only listen and imagine. Stacy defies the textbook description of a grandmother; she looks and acts young and energetic. She *is* young and energetic; I can say that because she has only a few years on me, and if I radiate only a smidge of the energy and youth she does in a few years, I'll be satisfied.

We speak of our families and the love we have for them, and she has more good news about her brother's continuing recovery. He was in a life-threatening vehicle accident about six months ago. He was not expected to live, but now he has his life back almost as normal as it was before. Life is a gift; neither of us need to be reminded of that. The things that matter most in life—in the Book of Life According to Kathleen—seem to be the things that matter to Stacy, too. She knows the value of precious time, loving family, and close friends. We are blessed with good health, affording us able minds and hands to work. Her hands have performed magic on my hair when I'm in a pinch. I have been devoted to a fabulous hairdresser for years, but when I have a hair emergency, Stacy is always there for me.

I assure her that if she ever needs speech therapy, I will be there for her. I hope she never does. We share a laugh and prepare to leave. If laughter makes us last, then she and I will be around for a long while.

STACY'S LUNCH DATES

"We will always do lunch in January!" Stacy, Shirley, and Denise said to each other as they moved on to their own independent salons after being employed together in a large salon. They had grown quite fond of each other, and they shared January birthdays.

They did have a birthday lunch every January for a number of years after they parted ways. It was their time-honored tradition but, somehow, it didn't last. Somehow, other things got in the way. It had been three years since they had had their January birthday lunch.

Because Stacy knows two heads are better than one—not just for haircuts, but for lunch dates, too—she invited both of them to be her lunch date(s). They met in January at *Cojitas*, a local, authentic Mexican restaurant. They celebrated their birthdays once again and, in Stacy's words, they had "lots of hair talk."

I've been in the hairstylist's chair enough times to know that they probably shared much deeper things than "hair talk." Deeper words and thoughts tend to flow when a hairstylist is in the group, and I'm sure this was multiplied times three. I wasn't privy to their conversation, but something tells me that whether or not they actually spoke the words, they all left their lunch date knowing that those we love and care about are what makes life so rich.

8/30: KATIE

There are many people who deserve special thanks for being there when I needed them in my time of loss. There were so many people who never left my side, and I will be forever grateful. They were my closest friends, and I hope I never have to repay the kindness in that form, but I would in a heartbeat.

There are two others who, while I didn't consider them my friends then, I do now. You will meet Theresa on October 13th. Today, you will meet Katie.

In those dark days, my work was that of the traveling therapist I mentioned in the introduction. I was a fleeting figure in all the facilities I served; I wasn't in any of them long enough to form close ties. Most people working in those buildings knew who I was, but I didn't think they knew much else. Some heard the news, I'm sure, but most people didn't know what to say. Most said nothing.

Katie knew what to say. She was a young social worker in one of the nursing facilities, and I didn't know her well. Her smile and kindness were disarming, and it was easy to accept her heartfelt sympathy. She was so young; how could she be so wise in knowing all the right things to say?

She didn't stop at just one measure of condolence. She continued to check up on me, making sure I was doing okay. I didn't know much about her, but I soon learned more, and I understood. She was preparing to lose *her* mom to cancer. Her mother passed away at the end of July after my parents died in March. She was already speaking the language of loss.

I will be forever grateful for her unyielding kindness in my time of need. I wasn't much comfort for her when she lost her mother, because I didn't know what she was going through. It wasn't until long after her mother died that I found out about her loss. Our bond strengthened; we have remained close.

She has a good start on being in the Boys Club. Her son, Kale, was one year old in May. If there are more children, I hope she remains the queen of the house like I am. We have other things in common, too. We both married builders, and today we compared our surprisingly similar upbringings. We discuss our life goals, and I see her at a point that I reached when I was about her age. She knows she wants to continue to work in a helping profession, but she isn't sure it is in her current situation.

She is 28 years old. I was naïve to the world of loss at her age, and she has already lost her mother. I had mine until I was almost 42 years old. She remains close to her father and her only sibling, an older brother. Life and loss have a way of spelling out the important things when a loved one is taken. She knows that time is a gift, and she isn't willing to bide it if she's not happy.

The facility she works in is just down the road from my office. Her lunch break is limited, so I suggest Christina's (July 22nd) idea: Lunch from Gourmet To Go in my office. She has never experienced it, either. Today's offering at GTG is a Greek pita sandwich, and I order two. They are a hit. My space here appears to be a hit with her, too.

My office is located in an historic building on "The Hill" in my small city. It served as the administration building of Marymount College until it closed in 1989. My 10'x12' expanse within it is a former faculty office. The building is now privately owned, with this half of the building housing offices, while the other side is currently being developed into residential condominiums. In between the two sides is the beautiful and ornate chapel, which once served as a church. Two of my husband's siblings were married there, as well as Kelly (January 22st) and her husband. They met while they were students here. Katie and I stand in this chapel and admire the splendor. The peace and calm are welcomed by us both. We didn't always feel it in our lives in the last few years, and now we recognize it quickly when it settles upon us, and without speaking it, we both know it is to be savored.

To say life is short, as I did in the first line of this book, is a simple understatement. What is not so simple is how to make the most of the time we have. At 45, I feel good about what I am doing to savor what I have been granted. At 28, Katie is light years ahead of me. I hope and pray I can repay her back for the kindness and insight she has given me. Perhaps I'll focus on paying it forward because, by her example, I think that is what I am supposed to do.

KATIE'S LUNCH DATE

You will meet my stepson on December 29th, my final lunch date of this project. I couldn't ask for a better young man to be a stepmother to. Katie, I'm sure, is the ideal stepdaughter. She has been one for several years, as her parents were divorced.

Katie had several ideas for her lunch date, but when I offered this guidance for her choice, she thought differently. Just like I told Rhonda several weeks ago, I told Katie this: *If this person died tomorrow, you'd never forgive yourself for not seeing them one last time.*

I have never acted as my stepson's mother. He has a mother in his life. I am his stepmother, and he calls me by my first name. I have never been a stepchild; I don't know how it feels. I know there must be some conflict of allegiance; when your mother is alive and present in your life, is it okay to be close to your stepmother? Is that fair to your mother? I had never thought about this set of conflicting emotions. As hard as it is sometimes to be a stepmother, I know it is harder to be a stepchild. I bow down to Katie and Matt for this dual role they didn't sign up for, but find themselves in. I didn't know much about Katie's stepmother until today.

Just like I was guilty of doing for so long before I launched this project, Katie would often tell her stepmother Sue this: "We should have lunch sometime." They never did. While Katie worked in the same town she lived in, their homes were about 40 minutes apart, and it was an extra effort. Katie decided this was the perfect reason to stop saying "we should," and make it happen.

As I'm sure they have done many times before in a figurative fashion, they *met in the middle.* They chose to dine at *El Puerto* in Abilene, Kansas, the same small town I dined in with Nancy on February 9th. Katie's son, Kale, was a guest as well. The restaurant was a sister to, and owned by, the same family as the *El Puerto* in my small city, where I dined with Anita in March and Christy in April. Our local *El Puerto* has since closed its doors and has been razed, making way for an expanded fast-food restaurant—the one with the great big yellow *M.*

Buildings go up and then come down; relationships do the same. If it is not meant to be, neither will stand the test of time. I feel blessed to have a harmonious relationship with my stepson, and Katie tells me today she sees her stepmother as a friend. Typically, the stepchild doesn't have much input towards their parent's choice when they remarry, so calling one's stepparent a *friend* is a high compliment. Sue is a lucky woman. I am a lucky woman, too.

9/3: GLORIA

When my high school class was planning our 20 year reunion, I polled several of my classmates with this question: "Who was your favorite grade schoolteacher?"

Hands down, and without hesitation, they all gave me the same answer: "Mrs. P." I knew it—they all felt the same way I did.

Gloria was my 4th grade teacher. As a 10-year-old girl, I thought she was hip and cool, and she was a nice teacher, to boot. She was married with a son a few years older than us so, of course, she seemed old. She was only 35 at the time.

That son, her only child, lives about 45 minutes from me. I didn't know this, so I took the long way around the job of finding her. I wanted to invite her to our reunion, and I wanted to surprise everyone. I heard through the grapevine she was living in California, and with a name like hers—I remembered her husband's name, too—she wasn't hard to find. Her husband, Ivan, answered the phone, but she wasn't home. He left her a note, and she said later that when she saw my name, she remembered me. I believe her. She wouldn't lie and set a bad example; she had to know I was still looking up to her. I really am looking up to her. I want to be like her when I grow up.

Mrs. P. is 70 years old, and she could easily pass for under 60. She is still hip and cool; I knew she would be when I invited her to our reunion. She showed up and surprised almost everyone—I leaked the big news to several people; I couldn't help it. She looks as young and vibrant as she did then because, at age ten, we all thought she must be at least 70 years old already. She was the biggest news there, because most of our small class of 18 has remained relatively close since graduation.

Since then, we have stayed in touch. She comes back to Kansas to visit her son and his family at least once a year, and we do all we can to make time for at least a short visit. She and Ivan no longer live in California. They retired, sold their home, and are traveling around the country, staying in a camper. They spend most of the year in Moab,

Utah, and winter in Quartzsite, Arizona. They remain active, hiking and walking nearly every day. They ride a Harley and go to the mecca in Sturgis, South Dakota, almost every year. She even has a small, tasteful tattoo on her ankle. *So* cool on her, if she can do it…. Her smile is still vibrant, and her blond hair is still pulled back. In short, she hasn't aged since 1976.

Her name was near the top on my very first list of 52 Lunch Dates, I assumed we would meet when she was in Kansas. Maybe not. She made a short trip to Kansas early in the summer for a family funeral, but I didn't get to see her then. Because Colorado Springs has beautiful scenery, hiking trails, *and* a skilled heart surgeon for Ivan, they are temporarily parked nearby in historic and beautiful Manitou Springs, Colorado, awaiting Ivan's September 12th date with the surgeon. Good thing they picked such a convenient location, because my sisters (Suzanne on December 28th, Gail on July 2nd) and I are traveling an hour past there on Labor Day weekend for our second annual sisters' getaway in Cripple Creek, Colorado. It is an old gold mining village-turned-gambler's haven nestled in the Rocky Mountains just behind Pike's Peak. Normally, I take my lunch dates out for a one-on-one so as not to take any attention away from them. However, this couldn't happen any other way. She may not make it back to Kansas after Ivan's surgery, and I can't risk that. She is far too dear to me. Gail and Suzanne don't seem to mind, either: I promised them more coverage in the book this way. This extra attention, I assured them, would make them even more memorable in the book. They felt pretty special about that.

One of the new traditions of the weekend is to go back down from the mountains into quaint and historic Manitou Springs to walk the sidewalks and take in the culture, with a certain stop at a certain gift shop for each of us to find a new Life is Good.® shirt, a theme we reinforce throughout the weekend. While this iconic brand is readily available in an independently owned store here, you will not find a single national franchise store in this enclave.

Mrs. P. is available to meet us for lunch on Saturday when we make the trip back into town. My sisters quickly recognize her on the crowded sidewalk as we drive through the crawling traffic. They didn't have her for a teacher, but they remember her.

"She still looks the same as she did then!" Suzanne said. We all agree on this one.

Parking is a cramped and crowded affair, but we find a spot up a side street and meet her on the sidewalk. It is always good to see her, and it is time to celebrate her as one of my *52 Lunches*. We wander a bit, aimlessly at first, not knowing which of the various restaurants to choose. The first choice requires a 45-minute wait, which is quickly ve-toed times four. The other side of the street appears to offer more op-tions, so we jaywalk across, just like everyone else does.

It was meant to be. The unassuming façade that houses *Coquette Creperie* holds Gail's first jackpot of the day. I explained Gail's intoler-ance to gluten in her chapter, and this restaurant happens to be gluten-free. The interior and staff are charming, and the food is savory, to say the least. The unique and delicious sandwiches they offer are wrapped inside a crepe, and we each pick the perfect one for our individual tastes. To quote Mrs. P., this place is "not your typical run-of-the-mill restaurant." The food almost parallels the company, and we let our-selves go into reverie about our hometown and the former students she remembers, even though she didn't teach either one of my sisters. She taught two of our four brothers, and while I know she would never speak an unkind word about them—or anyone—I'm pretty sure she didn't have any to offer. We laugh as we recall stories from our hometown and fill in the small memory gaps—ours, not hers— about the time she spent there.

And speaking of a good memory, she has other attributes that most 70-year-old women don't have. She remains youthful in her appear-ance, and when I ask her what the secret is, she replies that she was never afraid to try new things, and she still likes to travel.

"I feel good," she said, and it shows.

She arrived bearing a gift bag. "I feel so bad. You always remember my birthday, and I don't even know when yours is," she said.

By virtue of the fact that her birthday is the same day as two other friends, I remember to call her every year on May 25th. She hands me the bag, and inside is a book of poetry. Now, I am no poet, and I typi-cally don't even read poetry. However, just two days prior to this visit, I had a phone conversation with an artist from my small city. We talked about her art and my non-fiction writing, and she asked me if I ever attend the poetry reading series offered in a coffee shop there. Know-ing I need to expand my literary horizons, I made an informal com-mitment to give poetry another chance. Apparently, the teacher still knows what this student needs to learn.

I thank her, and she directs my attention to the card I overlooked in the bag. It is now framed and gracing an end table in my home. The front features a drawing of a young lady looking up, and the verse reads: *"If the only prayer you say your whole life is 'THANK YOU', that would suffice."* Could there be a more appropriate card for this entire *52 Lunches* project?   Again, she seems to know.

Mrs. P. decides to join us on the Life is Good. ® new shirt quest. She says she is not familiar with the brand, but I knew she would recognize it when she saw it, and she did. She joined in the fun, and she and I end up with matching shirts in the end. Nerdy, I know, but *so* cool for me.

I have a wonderful family, good health, and 52+ friends. At this very moment, Pikes Peak and its neighboring Rocky Mountains are enveloping the four of us in their awesome grandeur, and fresh, mountain air is filling my lungs and my head. I am in the company of three of the most amazing women I know. There was a point in my recent past when grief and sadness swallowed me whole. Right now, however, I feel surrounded by nothing but pure happiness. Life is good. For this certain awareness, I offer up a small prayer: *THANK YOU.*

GLORIA'S LUNCH DATE—as written by Gloria

The day is Tuesday, Nov. 22, 2011. It's almost Thanksgiving. My husband, Ivan, and I are in Quartzsite, AZ, where we spend the winter in our motorhome with thousands of other "snowbirds" from all over the US and Canada who've chosen to migrate south in search of sun and an alternative lifestyle. The desert awakens me with an incredibly beautiful sunrise, and I look forward to my lunch date with Tina, my desert neighbor from Idaho.

As I turn on the generator, TV, convection oven and hairdryer, I feel some guilt (and envy) that Tina is so content with so few material possessions. My focus today during our lunch will be to discover her recipe for the calmness and serenity she displays and her acceptance of people based on who they are, not how they compare to her. We've chosen a Mexican restaurant with outside seating. The sun is warm and relaxing.

Age 62, twice divorced, single, mother of four wonderful girls, Tina is the picture of health and is the most calm, stable person I know. Tina was raised in a small community with very few experiences outside of her immediate neighborhood. She remembers her mother "watering down the soup" to make it go around, while emphasizing to the children how "rich" they were as a family. The simplicity of her early life has translated into her adult life in a very positive way. Even though she has the money to live differently, she chooses this more "uncomplicated" way of life.

To quote her: "If you've never had or experienced something, you can live without it." She now resides in a 12' trailer, a small tent, no TV, no computer, no cell phone. The remainder of her belongings she sold or gave to her kids. It really takes very little to exist…She practices yoga, meditates daily and has taught herself to turn negative situations into positive ones. The sun, moon and stars are her guiding forces from which she absorbs energy and peace of mind. Metaphysical is how she describes herself.

Tina portrays all those things that we don't learn in books at school. Today she has been the teacher and I the student. From her I've learned the importance of acceptance, a positive mind set and good physical and mental health. Thanks, Tina, for being a daily reminder that "Life is good", and thanks, Kathleen, for providing the medium to make this day happen.

9/16: SHARON

If I'm in the middle of something when my home phone rings, I tend to ignore it. "If it's important," I think to myself as I let it ring, "they'll call my cell phone."

Three nights ago, I was cozied up in my bed, reading a good book. The phone rang, and I let it ring. My son brought it to me, and I rolled my eyes. Probably another telemarketer.

"Do you have your goals written down with a date set for reaching them?" the female voice said. I moved the phone from my ear and looked at it, like a genie may perhaps come out.

"Do you know who this is?" she continued. Sharon thought she was calling my cell phone.

I didn't. I am scared that perhaps this voice represents the spirit living in my head, reminding me that yes, indeed, I do need to set completion dates for several personal and professional goals I am working toward. I am really unnerved now, and a little scared. I really don't know who this is.

As good fortune and good timing would have it, I needed to hear these words I once spoke to the voice on the other end. Sharon took my words and made her dreams come true. Right now, I cannot see the forest for these trees I am lost in. These echoing words made a boomerang back to me at the perfect time.

"It's Sharon!" she says, as if I have just spaced out a significant chapter in my life—and hers. I am not quite lost in space, just floating outside the grasp of gravity. I feel bad for not recognizing her voice, but perhaps even worse for not recognizing the words that, according to her, set her on the wonderful path she now finds herself on.

In my work world, Sharon is a COTA—Certified Occupational Therapy Assistant. She helps her patients with 'ADLs', our lingo for Activities of Daily Living: getting dressed, brushing their teeth, and a myriad of other functions related to use of arms, hands, and visual perception are her focus. Until she left our mutual work setting in March of 2009, I was blessed to be on her therapy team in a local nursing home. She wasn't happy here, and I felt her pain. I sensed her difficulty, even though this facility was one of several I covered, and I didn't work but a few hours a week with her. It was long enough for her to make this impression on me: here is a spirited woman who needs to leave and find her way traveling to fulfill her dreams. I convinced her of this, and she packed her bags and hit the road as a traveling therapist. She had flirted with this notion but lacked the courage and conviction.

Sharon is single with two grown children, so she is at liberty to pull up stakes and go. She and her two dogs are the only beings she is responsible for now. She moved back to this area 14 years ago to take care of her mother. Coincidentally, she grew up in a small town next to my hometown, and we knew many of the same people. Our mothers were both from this small town as well; now they are neighbors again in Heaven.

When I was one year old and Sharon was 18, she was involved in a car accident in my hometown that took her fiancé and left her with severe injuries. She spent months convalescing on her own; there was no therapy offered for rehabilitation as there is now in our field. She learned the 'life is short' lesson earlier in life than I did. Most importantly, however, we both learned it.

Like my first lunch date, Jane Ann, Sharon wanted to be a hairdresser. She attended school in nearby Hays, home of my alma mater (go Fort Hays State Tigers!). It wasn't meant to be. She married and raised her children first, then graduated from her therapy training program in the same year I did in mine. After working several years, and after taking care of her mother, she moved to my small city, where our paths were destined to coincide.

Perhaps "once in a blue moon" a person like Sharon comes along. Maybe not even that often. Her energy and spirit are contagious, and tonight, at the Blue Moon in Minneapolis, Kansas, we celebrate the gift of our friendship.

Sharon was one of the rare few people who didn't forget my pain, not even months and years after my loss. She, too, was in 'The Club' as it is known, this exclusive society nobody wants to be in. The dues are extremely expensive, and they need only be paid once, although some people pay them multiple times. She called me every few months from her latest destination to see how I was holding out. She would thank me for her start on this new path, and I would accept her gratitude, but

I always felt I didn't have much to do with it. Tonight, she tells me she would have never left if not for me.

When she embarked on her journey, she went first to the Northwest. Oregon and Washington were her first stops, then on to Brownsville, Texas. She is now near Harlingen, Texas, just 30 miles from the coast of the Gulf of Mexico. She kept me posted on her whereabouts, but I must admit, I didn't make the effort to contact her like she did me. It had been some time since our last contact when my phone rang the other night, and here she was on a two-week assignment just two hours away. Better yet, she was staying with a friend just half an hour from me. I proposed the *52 Lunches* terms to her, and she agreed. She became the second lunch-turned-dinner date and, just like Kelley on May 4th, it couldn't happen any other way.

It was meant to be. She had never been to the Blue Moon, and it was halfway between us. It is a one-of-a-kind experience, tucked away in the bricked basement of an old Main Street building in this cozy town. The kitchen is open only on Friday nights. My husband, Mark, (May 13th), and our circle of friends are becoming regulars, and I had to invite him along because it is his favorite. He thanked me but declined, knowing I needed the time with Sharon.

Sharon's life bears little resemblance to her former existence just a few years ago. She sold her house, gave away or sold most of her belongings, keeping only her treasured antiques and keepsakes from her children's youths. Her blood pressure no longer needs to be medicated, and her motto is apparent in her interactions: "Leave a little happiness wherever you go."

We maximized the few hours we shared this evening; it was nearing closing time. We part ways, agreeing that we are blessed in so many ways. Just like I didn't realize it then, she has no idea how much she has inspired me to get moving on those dreams I hope to accomplish. The wheels in my head are turning, and I know what I have to do: I will set a time frame for those goals of mine, and I will write them down. I gave her permission to extend the timeline if necessary, so I'll do the same for myself.

"What if I'd never taken that first step?" she said. If she hadn't left, she would have never arrived in a better place. I'll be leaving soon; this I know for sure. My better place isn't somewhere else on the map, it is right here in front of me, ready for me to arrive. My old words came back first to haunt me, but now they are inspiring me through Sharon.

Perhaps I should answer the call when it comes, even if I *think* I am doing something more important.

SHARON'S DATE

The confirmation name I took when I was thirteen was "Margaret," so I like this girl already. Plus, she is planning on returning to college to become a speech therapist. Double jackpot. Margaret and Sharon shared a common work setting and both lost those jobs, leaning on each other throughout.

When Sharon interviewed for that job, Margaret was present. She recognized her because they had already met when they were walking their dogs.

Sharon is an occupational therapy assistant; Margaret is a speech therapy assistant. Sharon is licensed and qualified to work with both children and adults, Margaret is, too. However, because Medicare and most insurance companies don't pay for the services of a speech assistant—they pay for occupational and physical therapy assistants—the vast majority of them work in school settings or pediatric clinics. Their common work setting was in pediatrics.

I wish Margaret good luck and Godspeed in her endeavors to get into a graduate training program in speech language pathology. Admission is tight, and the competition can be tough. I will be honest in telling you that I did work hard to be granted a spot in graduate school, but lucky breaks don't hurt, either. Enough said.

Margaret is single with no children. She has considered adopting a child but is yet undecided. She is originally from Oregon and is hoping to attend graduate school there. Texas is not her home; she has no family there. She landed there after honorably serving our country in the Navy—thank you, Margaret, for your service. Sharon considers her family; they have chosen to spend some holidays together. Margaret invited Sharon to her church, and they enjoy worshiping together as well.

Sharon took her to lunch in November, dining at a favorite Greek restaurant. This whole project—paying it forward—is *not* Greek to Sharon. I don't know Margaret, but something tells me with a name and an occupation like hers, she's no stranger to the concept, either.

10/3: DENISE

Today's lunch is another first—times two. It is the first lunch date of the day when I actually had *two* lunch dates in one day, and it is the first lunch date who wants to take two different people to lunch at two different times because she can't decide on just one.

Before you meet Denise, however, I want to take you back just a bit. Remember on August 8th when I told you I loved my average Jane car, and I was so happy to get her back? Well, I was.

"Jane" is actually a Volkswagen Jetta, and it's only now as I type these words that I have named her this. Like the most common-colored car in America, she is silver. She truly is average, but average is good, and I love her. I always loved her, and I will always love her. However, Jane isn't destined to live forever; I realize this. Today, after this lunch, I must make a decision. I must decide, in therapy lingo, to rehab her, or send her to hospice care. She now needs care that might perhaps be beyond practicality, given her high mileage. I am so torn.

I brought her to a VW dealer in Wichita, Kansas, because they are the closest service professionals specializing in this German treasure. They kept her over the weekend and let me drive home a shiny, used, red VW Passat, a slightly bigger car that will accommodate my husband's long legs and my sons' growing bodies. Oh, and she, too, is beautiful. They knew when they let me take her home that I probably wouldn't be able to walk away from her. After this lunch, I will go back to see Jane. I will make my decision then. I think you are able to predict the future from here.

Denise was, and still is, a dear friend. She and I, along with Marilyn (June 14th) and Tracy (November 20th), were roommates in college. Tracy and I grew up together, and Denise and Marilyn grew up together. We lived for one year in a two-bedroom apartment. That was 26 years ago. Through thin and thick, through marriages, divorces, births and deaths, we have remained friends. I am so blessed.

Denise works for a fire and disaster restoration company. She is their marketing agent, spreading the word like fire about what her company can do in your time of need. She recently moved close to Wichita and is now geographically closer to her mother—a dear, sweet woman who would still, at age 84, do anything for her 11 children. She has already let go of three of them, as well as their father. Denise and I are in the club.

Denise has two children, a 20-year-old daughter who attends Kansas University in Lawrence, and an 18-year-old son who is a senior in high school. She is divorced from their father but has found a good man to keep her warm, inside and out. Not that she wanted it, but I easily gave him my stamp of approval not long after I met him.

"It's easy with him," she says. That is apparent. They just returned from a trip to Jamaica in August.

We meet today at Harry's Uptown, a local favorite bar and grill in downtown Wichita. Her office is just outside of Wichita, but she travels a wide radius around south-central Kansas. Today she is in town, and the timing is perfect. We grab a patio table to take advantage of this beautiful Indian Summer Day. She orders a BLT, and I order fish and fries. Both are sinfully delicious.

We enjoy the sunshine on our faces and talk about the sunny days we find ourselves living in lately. We haven't both always been this content with our lives: she struggled as a single mother, and she struggled to let go of her father and her siblings.

Our 26-year-old friendship has waxed and waned, but never faded away. In the last few years, however, we have committed ourselves to keeping in closer touch. She has a sister living in my small city, so we make sure to combine visits whenever possible.

So, few things in life are permanent, we both know this well. Tattoos, however, are permanent. She is considering getting two small, tasteful tattoos, one to honor her maiden name and her mother with initials and birthstones, and another to honor her love of running. Again, like Mrs. P. exactly one month ago today, they make me think: "Hmm. If *they* can do it...."

Like me, she is a running junkie. We took a running class together while in college, but neither of us felt the passion for it then like we do now. We agree it has saved our lives when we had to let go of our loved ones.

There is a theory that states something like this: The qualities—good or bad—you identify in others are representative of your own qualities. You recognize them because you have them. Today, Denise tells me I am kind and broadminded. You spot it, dear Denise, you got it. I could go on to share more of her positive qualities with you, but given this theory, that might make me look like I'm bragging on myself. I'll just say she is a friend I am so lucky to have.

DENISE'S LUNCH DATE—as written by Denise

Let's just say, my "times two" didn't come to fruition. I waited too long after Kath's and my lunch date, and the end of 2011 was rapidly approaching. Attempts were made on my part to schedule with my friend in Sterling, but to no avail.

Enough about my missed opportunity. Let's move forward to my evening "lunch" date. It's Friday, December 16th, 2011, and it's a clear, beautiful start to a great weekend! You see, after I finish my "lunch," my baby girl (okay, she's a junior at KU) is arriving home for winter break tonight. My lunch date and I are meeting at Doc Green's in New Market Square on Maize Road in Wichita. Deb(ra) and I met and became fast friends at good ole' FHSU (Fort Hays State University) in the mid 80's. While distance (she lived in Denver, CO, briefly after college) and family commitments didn't/don't always allow us to see one another often, when we do reconnect, we pick right back up…not exactly where we left off, but we always manage to get caught up, and it's an easy, comfortable experience that we begin and end with a hug.

Aside from running into one another while having lunch in the same restaurant (with different lunch dates) in April 2011, we hadn't seen each other since we got together for coffee in Hutchinson, KS, in 2009. Deb shows up at Doc Green's with a big, beautiful smile and a laugh to match. As we talk of our children, both the smile and laugh show up often. Starting in January 2012, all three of her young adult children will be attending college. She has two sons and one daughter.

Let's jump back to good ole' FHSU. I remember "children/family" being a back-burner life experience for Deb. An English major, she was/is a fabulous writer, and her life was headed in the career direction. In walks Alan, shortly before she finishes college. Then, early in her career, "family" moves to the front burner. They are a family strong in faith, and Deb home-schooled all three children. One other word to describe Deb, along with her beautiful smile and laugh, is *dedicated*.

During our "lunch," we talked of a teaching opportunity in her near future with a local school district in Maize, KS. (Fingers crossed!) We talk of my job, based out of Maize, and what a small world it is. If I know Deb, she will transition beautifully from dedicated, full-time spouse and parent to dedicated full-time spouse and teacher, or whatever life has in store for her.

There is mention of those in our lives whom we love and have lost (my dad and her mom). She asks about my beautiful mother, and like all who know my mother, she mentions what a sweet, amazing woman she is.

It's hard to believe we can catch up in a couple of hours. However, it's time to go catch up with one of the loves of my life, waiting at my home, ready for her mama (me!) and the bottle of wine I'm bringing.

Note: Even though my "times two" lunch date didn't occur, this fabulous idea of Kath's…pay it forward…has inspired me to reach out to a friend who moved her family to the Wichita area to allow her sons more opportunity. We are beginning to rekindle our long-time friendship. (This friend was the kindergarten teacher for both of my children.)

10/3 (EVENING MEAL): LOIS

I left Denise after what seemed like a brief lunchtime always flies when there isn't enough of it to spend with old friends. I proceeded to the east side of Wichita to make my decision. I was armed with my dad's bargaining skills and the knowledge that my mother's favorite color was red. I warned the sales manager that, after buying a car by myself as a college student, the dealer told me this: "If every woman could buy a car like you, they wouldn't need men to help them." Another dealer offered me a job after my husband and I bought a car from him. While I am small in stature (like my mother), my negotiating skills are mighty (like my father).

Walking back into the VW dealer's office with my jaw squarely set, I was ready to give them my top dollar. They had their bottom dollar ready, and we ended up meeting in the middle. They treated me well, compensating for the sacrifice I agreed to in other forms of VW currency. Knowing they would be proud of my purchase *and* my acumen with car dealers, I drew from my parents' remaining endowment, wrote a check for the red Passat, told Jane I would always love her, and didn't look back—I couldn't bear to. I do love my new car, though. I have named her Scarlett.

My friend, Lois, then proceeded to meet me in the middle. I traveled a few more miles east, she drove west about 20 miles, and we met at Applebee's in Andover, Kansas. She told her husband she was having dinner with me because I was in Wichita buying a car.

"She bought a car all by herself?" her husband asked, apparently in disbelief.

"You don't know Kathleen," she said back to him with a laugh.

She does know me. I love Lois for so many reasons, one of them being that she leaves me feeling like a million bucks. She always has. Lois is old enough to be my mother, because she is the same age as my mother would have been. And speaking of birthdays, here's the coolest thing about Lois: she is my birthday buddy—we share April 17th as the day we both entered the world.

I met Lois in the fall of 1988. I was a green, naïve new college graduate. I had just graduated with a bachelor's degree in sociology, and I was kicking off the first of many short-term work stints until I returned to college four years later to obtain my master's degree. I refer to those years as my "gypsy days," but I have no regrets because I met wonderful people like Amy (July13th), and Lois, and tasted so many different flavors of life I wouldn't otherwise have if I'd followed the well-worn path.

Lois has retired and now spends her time with her husband, her three children and three grandchildren. Retirement hasn't slowed her down; she has traveled extensively far and near and is preparing to take her entire family on a Caribbean cruise next June to celebrate their 50th wedding anniversary. She and her husband recently traveled to New Zealand with another couple and took an Alaskan cruise four years ago.

Closer to home, she finds contentment in day trips with her family to the scenic Flint Hills nearby, where she and her family own 827 acres of land. This land was homesteaded by Lois's grandmother when she came to Kansas in a covered wagon. Their land boasts a lake, providing them with catfish, crappie, and bass fishing enjoyment. Lois related the enjoyment of her grandmother's stories of the Native Americans she encountered there. As a child, these stories captivated Lois, and she has carried them with her since.

In nearby Matfield Green, Kansas, the Flint Hills carry more charms in the form of the annual Prairie Chicken Dance. In order to partake of this local spring event, Lois got up at 3:00 a.m. because animal mating rituals such as this don't take the human sleep cycle into consideration. She attended for the first time this year; it was one of those things she felt she must do. Perhaps I'll go with her next year, but the thought of half a night's sleep doesn't beckon me at this point. I'll settle for another dinner with her instead, and more simple forms of birdwatching.

She and I speak at least once each year on April 17th, but I realize even more today this is not enough. Like Dot (December 6th) and Ila (March 12th), Lois is a motherly companion, but yet we are peers, too. I want to bottle up some of her quiet energy and earthy motherly-ness and take it with me, but it can only be felt in her presence, so I savor it as I savor my last few bites.

We finish our dinners and proceed to the parking lot so I can show off Scarlett to her. She is impressed, smiling, oohing, and marveling at my beautiful red car. My mother would have marveled, too. Today, I will choose to believe that Mom is smiling upon her daughter and her new car. I'm pretty sure she has asked Lois to stand in for her on Earth today to show me how much she loves my car, and how much she still loves me, too.

LOIS'S LUNCH DATE—as written by Lois

I met Janet at a class reunion in 1963. She went to school with my sister-in-law and my husband. I would see her every two years at high school class reunions, but we became friends in 1976 when we moved from Wichita to a nearby small town. This was the hometown of my husband and also the location of the high school class reunions. Janet and her family had always lived in the area where the reunions were held.

My husband and I have three children, and Janet and her husband had two children the same age as our two older children. Our children became good friends with Janet's children and went to school together until they graduated from high school.

Janet's youngest son and our middle son became great friends and had many wonderful adventures. The boys loved going to the country and always enjoyed the 4-H activities—getting the lambs ready for the fair, playing with the farm animals, and doing country activities. Janet's son spent time staying at our home doing all the fun town activities. Snow skiing in the winter was another great adventure the boys enjoyed together.

During this time, Janet and I became really good friends and enjoyed spending time together during the years our children were in school together. I started working away from home when my children were in junior high and high school, and I was very busy. Our children graduated from high school and left home, and my life changed dramatically. Janet moved to a country home farther away from mine, and we drifted apart. We were always eager to visit at the reunions or a small-town event, but our time together was limited.

Several years later I was able to retire, and when I was encouraged to renew a friendship (thanks to Kathleen), I knew I wanted it to be with Janet. She had had many changes in her life, too, and had moved to another town. We lived closer together again with that move, which made it easy to renew our friendship. She was eager to have lunch together, and we had a wonderful visit. We decided to enjoy more activities together. We now belong to a club that meets once a month and are both active in doing club-related functions. It is wonderful to visit and keep in touch at least two times a month.

Friendships are so precious. Thank you for the encouragement you gave me to renew a great friendship.

10/13: THERESA

If the administrative staff at Smoky Hill Rehabilitation Center would have left it up to me to decide upon the Employee of the Year, I would have picked Theresa, but they didn't ask me. They went ahead and chose her anyway. Without sounding sappy and overbearing, let me just say this: she has a heart of pure gold, a heart suited perfectly for nursing critically- and terminally ill adults.

Theresa is a registered nurse at one of the handful of facilities I now work at. As the "treatment nurse," she treats the residents' wounds and injuries, among other duties. This is not our first common workplace. We met at the local hospital about six years ago, and we both moved on to other settings.

Like Katie on August 30th, Theresa seemed to have mastered the language of loss when I was just learning it. She reached out to me, moving earth and heaven to try to make my pain lessen even a bit. At that time, she was working at a nursing home I was covering for another therapist, and she did backbends to make my work in her facility as effortless as possible, knowing that grief doesn't always allow clear thinking on the job.

She didn't stop there. I would go on to see her two other times in public places, and both times she extended a heartfelt, "How are you?" Her tone implied not a cursory greeting, but a true concern for my well-being.

After the second time she asked, I knew: "You've been here, haven't you?" I asked.

"Yes," she said with a kind and knowing smile.

Theresa's mother passed away fifteen years ago. She was battling cancer and then suffered a stroke. She was 45. Teresa was 19. Her mother was perfect, just like mine. She remains close to her two sisters and her farmer father, who is perfect, too, just like my farmer father was. She has been speaking this language a lot longer than I have. She knows when to speak it, and when to keep it silent. Today, however, she and I speak it fluently during this lunch.

Whenever I see Theresa at her work—which is almost daily, lucky me—I want to speak this language with her. I want to stop whatever I am doing and ask her to do the same, and simply share our common bond. I realize, even more today, that we don't need to talk about it every time we see each other because we both know it inside and out. Our smiles in passing convey this. I have come to the painful realization that, unfortunately, one doesn't speak or understand this language unless you have experienced profound loss. I want every person I know to understand this language, but I don't want them to suffer the required loss. I realize I didn't understand or speak it before my loss. To anyone I didn't comfort or reach out to in your time of loss before mine, I want to issue this public apology: I am so sorry. I didn't know what to say and, more importantly, I didn't know it is okay not to know what to say. It is most important to let the grieving person know you are there, whether or not there is anything that can be said or done at that moment.

Today, I ask her if she is comfortable talking about her mother, and she says 'yes' and that she likes to talk about her. I like to talk about my parents, too. However, I have found, too, that unless my listener knows this breed of loss, they aren't quite as comfortable talking about it with me. They don't want to cause me any apparent pain. I want these people to know that even if I seem upset, or if I cry a little, that's okay. Theresa and I both get a little teary as we talk, but that really is okay, and neither of us have to acknowledge this. We already know.

Theresa is the mother of Caitlyn, a thirteen-year-old girl named in honor of the grandmother she never knew named Catherine. Theresa has been a single mother all of her daughter's life, but she will soon be a married mother of four children when she becomes a stepmother to her fiancé's children after they celebrate their vows in the spring. Her joy and excitement is obvious.

I married my husband one week after I completed college and had our boys three and six years later. Their dad has always been present, active and devoted. It was challenging to complete college as a single woman and challenging in another way to mother two sons with their dad. Theresa did all this as a single mother. I cannot imagine—really, I cannot. I bow down to her even more. As if she doesn't already seem Herculean in her strength, let me share this with you, because she said I could: six years ago, she was diagnosed with Hodgkin's lymphoma. She has been cancer-free for five years.

We speak today of the sure knowledge that life is, indeed, too short, and we both want to maximize our opportunities here to extract all the happiness we can with whatever time we have been granted. I share with her that I want to be a writer when I grow up, but at this point my work as a speech therapist keeps me from being a starving artist. She confirms that yes, just as it appears, she loves being a nurse. Perhaps not forever, but she loves what she does, and it shows. She wasn't chosen as Employee of the Year on a whim: her dedication is apparent.

True to her temperament, she wanted to choose a restaurant I, too, would like. I didn't offer any suggestions (remember, I gave that up at the halfway point), yet she still chose my favorite fare: Mexican food at Cojitas, an authentic, locally owned restaurant I hadn't yet visited. The food was divine, and the service was superb. The staff spoke their language, and we spoke ours. I didn't understand theirs, and I don't know if they picked up on ours, but I know this: Theresa and I share a loss that defies the spoken word. Just as the pain of loss has no words to fully describe its depth, neither does the bond of mutual understanding I feel with her. There are no words strong enough for that, either—and I ought to know, because I make my living with the spoken word.

One of my mother's favorite saints was Saint Theresa. I think I have my very own Saint Theresa now.

THERESA'S LUNCH DATE

Because our small city is just that—a small town, actually—there is a lot of overlap between my lunch dates and *their* lunch dates. I know some of them. I knew Theresa's date in a professional capacity for several years. Our paths crossed in that manner because Glenn is a prosthetics/orthotics technician. This means he fits people with artificial limbs and braces for impaired limbs. Our paths did literally cross many times in the hallways of the hospital when I worked there, as well as the multiple nursing homes we both saw patients at. He was always friendly and welcoming.

Glenn just happens to have the same last name as my grandmother's maiden name, and it is not common. We compared notes; perhaps somewhere *way* back there is a connection, who knows. It doesn't matter because we are all connected somehow. We used to be connected through the hospital, but my good marriage at that job was a jig whose time was up: It was good while it lasted. Now I see him at the facility where Theresa works—I am there frequently, too, and he is friendly and kind, as usual. Theresa works closely with him at this facility when he comes to see a resident because she is the Treatment Nurse—that means she fixes things on patients' bodies whenever she can. Glenn helps with that, providing consultation for braces, orthotics and in some cases, artificial limbs. Theresa fixes the things she can, and when she can't, Glenn provides compensations. She always tries to fix their broken hearts and souls too, if necessary.

Because nursing home nurses are typically tending to residents' needs with very little time to spare, Theresa took the opportunity to treat Glenn to lunch to let him know how much she values his professional support, always delivered with a kind, warm-hearted touch to those in need.

There are some things in life that can't be fixed: we all know this. When someone who is as quietly strong and visibly kind as both Glenn and Theresa are, and they are able to make it better in some way, I call that a gift.

10/26: KRISTIE

When I was a kid, the Schwan man visited our house regularly. He was mysterious in a cool, magical way. He drove that big truck all the way out to our farm, and it was as if it came straight from Heaven's kitchen. It was refrigerated and stocked with the most extraordinary ice cream treats and other frozen foods. When he pulled in the driveway, it was always a special day. As children, we never had much extra, but we always had enough. And food, well, *that* was the highest priority. My six siblings and I were always ready to eat, and our parents always fed us well. The Schwan man was responsible for so much of that good food, and now when I see that familiar earth-toned truck, I feel satisfied in my stomach and in my heart.

As a farm girl, I always knew food came from the earth, but this food had to come from somewhere very special on the earth. Someone very smart and insightful had to know how to create such pleasurable ice cream flavors and knew just the right spices to put in the frozen burritos. I even liked to eat their frozen vegetables. I wanted to know who these people were who created such tasteful treats.

Today, I am having lunch with one of those brilliant people. Kristie is a food scientist for the Schwan's corporation in my small city. She is also identified as a "super taster," which means that she must possess an extraordinarily high number of taste buds in order to sense subtle tastes that others may not taste. What a bonus—she was already their scientist when testing revealed this gift.

Today we pleasure our taste buds with sushi. I have enjoyed it only several times in my life, so I need a little assistance determining my preference, and she is just the one to help me because she is a regular here at the Daimaru Steak House. But enough about food—this is about our friendship.

I haven't seen Kristie in more than a year; I am not proud of this. It has been a difficult year for her, but she is moving forward. Like Gail on January 30th, Kristie has just gone through a divorce. And, like Gail, she was married to one of my husband's friends. Finally, like Gail, my husband and I want to keep both halves of this former couple as our friends. It could happen no other way. We still love them both, and we refuse to shut either of them out. They have all agreed to stay with us. Yet another similarity is that she has two boys—like Gail and me, too.

Just as it was with Gail and her ex-husband, Kristie's ex-husband and my husband maintained their friendship in a relatively seamless manner after the divorce. I cannot claim the same, as I illustrated in Gail's chapter. I will take the blame for not reaching out when they were going through those dark days. I will use the word—and I hate this word—that Kristie used today about re-establishing our relationship: "awkward." I knew both Gail and Kristie were struggling, and I knew that in time we would eventually connect again, but too much time passed. Too much opportunity was lost to celebrate our friendship. I find out today that it is never too late.

I haven't experienced the loss and devastation of divorce, but loss is loss, and I know the depths of darkness you can find yourself in when life plunges you into a painful, unfamiliar place. I should have been there in her struggles, but we agree to move forward from this point.

Even though it had been a about a year, I remember her smile. Today, however, that smile is replaced by a brighter, more genuine smile. She looks happy. She confirms that she is.

"I want to relax and enjoy life. I didn't give myself a chance to do that for a long time," she says. She has a new man in her life, and I can see this is a good thing. "My mom tells me she is seeing 'the old Kristie that I used to know!'"

Kristie's official work title is "Senior Product Development Manager." She supervises seven people. Her degree in bakery science, along with her natural sense of leadership, qualified her for this position. She enjoys her job and tells me that her leadership and management training help her in her personal life, too.

"I've learned to recognize my strengths." She says she has needed them for her personal life lately, but her calm demeanor today belies this. "I use mental talk to realize what is important."

What is most important is her membership in the Boys Club. Her two sons qualify her for this exclusive clique. Connor is ten years old, and Ethan is almost eight. We share stories of the wonders and woes of boys; neither of us would have it any other way.

Kristie is too humble to agree with this, but she is stunningly beautiful in a calm, quiet way. Her tastes in fashion match mine, and I am lucky to be her size because she has bestowed some of her cast-offs upon me, and I am so thankful. One article of clothing I don't expect to inherit is this: she now wears a Boy Scout-brown button-down shirt as the official den leader of her son's Webelos group. She says perhaps she'll "bedazzle" it to give it a little life, because it isn't her style.

I feel a kinship with her as the mother of only boys, but more than that, we understand each other as women. Our lives don't have many parallels on the surface besides motherhood, but sometimes that is what makes it tick. I don't know her pain, and she doesn't know mine. I come from a family of seven and she has one sibling. She works full-time plus; I am a slacker compared to her. She likes to cook; I don't.

Below the surface, however, is where it matters, and if she's in it for the long haul, I plan to keep her around as my friend for as long as both of us live and breathe. We are both at places in our lives where we feel more happiness than ever before. Perhaps that is the only similarity that matters right now.

KRISTIE'S LUNCH 'DATE'

There were a handful of lunch dates in this project that I knew I needed to follow-up with, people who were so important to me. People who, perhaps, paid it forward, but I didn't reach back out to collect their story. People I wanted to stay close to, but time and circumstance got in the way.

I hate to admit it, but I think this is what went down after my first lunch date with Kristie. I slacked, the project lagged, and the months and years went by. Kristie and I continued to live our own lives, and life went on for both of us.

I would see her in passing—at the grocery store, running errands, even in the cemetery once when she was walking her dog and I was running while I was in town. I would always say those same dreadful words: *"We need to get together again,"* and, *"I'm still working on that lunch date book. I AM going to finish it someday."* And then it ended there. Again. Ugh.

The day after I met with my cover artist, and just a few short weeks before I finally did finish this book, I saw her at an outdoor concert in the downtown of our small city. I had had enough of my own excuses, and I took matters in my own hands again and broke my own rules again. After a warm exchange first of pleasantries, followed by a meaningful conversation like the ones we once had, I knew that her "lunch date" needed to be with me once again. I had stepped away from our conversation for a moment when another acquaintance of hers approached her and engaged in small talk, and in those few minutes, I heard my little voice screaming once again: *"Make a date NOW. And make it for sooner, rather than later. Stop the 'we should…'"*

So, the day after Mother's Day, two days after that concert, and just before I finally finished his book, we met for lunch. At the same restaurant we met for our first lunch, but this time it had moved to the other end of town, closer to her work. We were able to talk like we used to; we wasted no time getting the heart of our matters, the same matters that have always brought us together. We understand each other, and we held nothing back. We connected on the same level, just eleven years later. Perhaps even easier, because, as we are both now over fifty, we realize how important our friends are. We realize they are a lifeline, not a luxury as they once were when we were singly focused on motherhood, because we felt there was no other way.

Now, our five sons are all legal adults and making their own decisions. Some are near and some are far, but we know we are now passively mothering at best.

It's about us now, it's our turn to make our lives what we want to make them. Kristie has moved forward in that process, and while I am still trying to acclimate to our empty nest, I am moving forward, too.

I came home from an awesome garage sale last weekend with a cool vest. It was long and loose and designed for active wear. While I was trying it on in front of our bedroom mirror, my husband noticed, and called it a nice "smock."

"It's a vest, not a smock," I told him. "Besides, we don't even use that word anymore." I rolled my eyes at his attempted humor and threw it in the laundry basket to get it ready for its maiden outing.

At the close of our lunch today, Kristie collected her phone and glasses from the table, preparing to leave. "I have to go back and head out to the plant. I have to put on a hair net and a smock."

I laughed and told her the story. She laughed, too. She gets it. She always has. And if that's what it takes to continue to make those delicious treats to fill the brown truck, then a smock it is.

11/11: PEGGY

Today is Stacy's (August 22nd) lucky day—eleven is her lucky number--and in so many ways, it is mine, too. I am dining with Peggy today, and coincidentally, I met Peggy through Stacy and Gail (January 8th). She was their friend before she was mine. For this introduction, I am thankful to both of them.

If my mother's meal preparation resulted in a plate of food that was all the same color, she would groan and acknowledge this lack of color. I am groaning, too, and acknowledging the lack of color among my lunch dates—until today. Peggy is Black. I wish my circle of friends was less racially homogenous and more colorful. Nutritionists tell us that a more colorful plate is healthier. I believe a more colorful array of friends is healthier, too. My mother would agree on both counts.

A mother never wants to acknowledge this possibility, but I told Peggy today that if anything were to happen to me, she would be my first choice as a new mother for my boys. Peggy is single and has no children, but she is highly qualified. I have seen her with my boys—hands down, she's got the job.

She could keep my boys in line because her job is that of a probation officer. Plus, she would handle them with tender love and care.

"The parole officer's job is to keep people from going back to jail: mine is to keep them out of jail," she says, explaining the difference between the two jobs. Peggy has a quietly strong personality; I can see that she is well-suited for this position. She could surely keep my boys out of jail.

We dine today at Carlos O'Kelly's, my second lunch date here—her choice. I dined with Nancy here on February 9th. I worked here when I arrived in 1991. I landed here because I was coming down from my year in Philadelphia where I met Amy (July 13th), and I needed a job. I had my bachelor's degree in sociology, which suited me well in waitressing. (It didn't seem to suit me for much else.)

Peggy arrived in our small city in 1985. She was recruited by the very college whose building houses my office. She played basketball and volleyball for the former Marymount College. She came from Memphis, Tennessee, and thought she'd never get used to such a small town. I came from a dot on the map and thought perhaps this town was too big. She didn't plan on staying—neither did I—but the town does grow on you if you let it.

She spent one year at a junior college in southeast Kansas as an athlete. She spent the remainder of her college career at Marymount, and hasn't left Salina—for good, anyway. She does travel the 10-plus hours home to Memphis to see her parents and three siblings about once every year. She knows the importance of family. Maybe that's why I have always been drawn to her—she *gets* it. She understands what is important in life, and what is not. This is apparent after spending a short amount of time with her after you meet her. She has that *something*—that calm sense of peace that can easily erupt into infectious laughter that makes you want to laugh, too. Then, you just want to hang with her and soak up more of her spirit. She gives it away easily, but apparently, she can make more because she always has more to give the next time you see her.

She has a vibrant smile that sets well on her beautiful ebony complexion, and she shares this smile freely, too. When she smiles and laughs, there is a magnetism that pulls you in. It cannot be described in words, but it is there. Some people have it, and you know because you get drawn in—in a good way.

My mother had it, too, but unlike Peggy, she was quiet. Peggy never met my mom or my dad. Yet, she came to my house with Bob and Stacy for dinner several weeks after my parents died. They sat at the dining room table with us and listened to stories about two people they didn't know. Peggy gave us that smile, and it brought me a small but meaningful measure of peace at this dark time in my life. My mother, I'm sure, was looking down and smiling her big, vibrant smile at this colorful dinner I was being served.

PEGGY'S LUNCH DATE

Peggy is a woman of great faith, which she practices weekly at her church with a circle of friends she has formed there. In her usual way, she formed friendships there easily, and in the usual human way, too many of these friendships are not celebrated as much as they should be. The shopping dates aren't fulfilled, the visits aren't made, and, more specifically for the purposes of this book, the lunch dates never happen. And then, it becomes harder. People move away or go to another church.

Peggy had a friend who no longer goes to her church but did join another local church. Because she no longer saw her in church, she made the effort to reach out to her in order to connect again, and they have renewed their friendship through frequent evenings out.

In the many months it has taken to complete this project, Peggy has become a member of "The Club." She lost her mother after a long illness. If I had a secret for overcoming the grief, I would share it with her. If I had been granted a magic wand to take away other people's grief, I would use it on her. I don't have any of those powers, and I know her pain. I know, however, that the faith that led her to her friend in church is continually leading her to peace with her mother's passing. It is always a journey and never a destination; we simply keep moving forward through the pain, but it never goes away.

Peggy, like me, is at peace with that.

11/18: KATE

If I get into any legal trouble in the near future, I hope it is after my niece Kate graduates from law school. I pity the person on the other side of the story if she is the attorney. As proof that I'm not simply a biased aunt, let me state this fact: She is the first person in her class of 156 at Washburn University to have a job waiting for her after her graduation next spring.

I stated in the introduction that this book wouldn't be possible without the inspiration from my parents. Her law school endeavor wouldn't have come to fruition without the same inspiration from her grandparents, my parents. Kate is Gail's (July 2nd) daughter, older sister to Abby (May 25th).

We are having "lunch" at 4:45 p.m. today. I am on my way to Kansas City, and her plan was to meet over the noon hour in Topeka because she was free when we made plans. She was called to court for class, so I was "forced" to shop to pass the time. How dreadful for me. Because I rarely miss any meals at regular feeding times, and because she made me wait, I took the liberty of choosing a Mexican restaurant when she gave me the choice, even though I swore I'd never do that again right after her sister's date. We are dining at On the Border. The chips and salsa arrived before she did, thus saving my life. I indulge, and she talks. She's good at that, and what she says is packed with meaning. She uses words like "discretion" and "utility." She is going to be a good attorney.

She tells me today that she was intrigued by the framed Bill of Rights on the wall at her third- grade friend's house. Her friend's father was an attorney.

Throughout hers and Abby's childhood, they spent a lot of time on the farm with my parents. My mother, the Great Encourager, made sure Kate knew this as she matured through her teenage years: "You carry yourself well, and you speak well." Kate never forgot this inspiration from her grandmother. Nor did she forget The Bill of Rights on her friend's wall.

At her grandparents' funeral, Kate met Nancy, who was a grade-school friend of her mother's. Nancy had moved away to my small city when she and Gail were in the eighth grade. Nancy is now a Kansas Supreme Court Justice. Kate had kept the idea of law school churning on low, and at the time of the funeral she was in retail management after completing her bachelor's degree at Kansas State University.

The turning point came in April after the funeral in March. Her co-worker and friend, Jason, told her this: "All the tears in the world won't bring your grandparents back. Do something to carry on their legacy."

Jason took his life that same month. As a young gay man, his struggles overcame his strength. Kate took the LSAT (Law School Admission Test) in October—a law school prerequisite and began law school the next fall. Kate established a scholarship fund in Jason's name at Washburn University in Topeka, Kansas, after an intensive fundraising campaign through the Gay and Lesbian Alliance to honor his memory and to carry on his legacy. He was never a student there, but Kate was—thanks to him and her grandparents.

Despite her busy schedule as a Kansas Supreme Court Judge, Nancy agreed—with her characteristic enthusiasm—to be Kate's mentor in law school. Kate accepts her input but does her part as well. Kate's work ethic parallels her mother's, and it has impressed her teachers and employers since her inception into law school. The comments made in awe of her high energy level are countered by Kate's tribute to her mother and grandparents: "I grew up watching Mom work so hard to support me and my sister as a single mother. I spent a lot of time on my grandparents' farm growing up. I know how to work." She makes me look like a slacker which, in comparison, I am. I am fantasizing about settling into semi-retirement as I work on becoming a writer.

Kate was hired by the firm in Wichita that provided her with an internship last summer. She is currently interning with a firm in Topeka, where, as a law clerk, she proved a veteran lawyer with 25 years of experience *wrong*. Yes, *wrong*. She found a listed, but unpublished, opinion from the Kansas Court of Appeals, thus saving his firm $75,000. After he swallowed his pride and acknowledged his error, he offered her a job. She was already taken.

Kate's academic success is eclipsed only by the real-life lessons she has been taught from loss and law school. She tells me she feels she has learned how to stand up for herself, as well as how to be responsible. I always thought she was standing pretty much erect before. Kate is single and without children, but she has a treasured terrier. She hasn't let any of these tough lessons in her life change her perspective. "I feel so blessed every day," she says.

Kate towers over me by eight inches. Sometimes, both literally and figuratively, the aunt looks up to the niece. I feel blessed every day, too. We see eye-to-eye on that one.

KATE'S LUNCH DATE

This lunch date was the last one I collected, and it was well worth the wait. Kate had told me for some time that she was struggling to write this story, because she wanted it to be absolutely perfect.

"It will be perfect, no matter what," I assured her. Still, she struggled.

In the end, we wrote it together, and I think it is one of, if not the most perfect lunch date story. But I am a bit biased.

Her lunch date was not one lunch date, but a series of lunches and dinners with someone she had known all her life, but knew she needed to connect with, and get to know as an adult. Her "date" is 13 years younger than her; her cousin, Jude.

Jude is my firstborn son.

Kate and Jude have known each other since they were young but are now adults. They always enjoyed a cousin relationship, and they still do, but now they are both adults, and have the gift of a friendship as well.

"He is the first cousin I have known since the beginning of their lives. I was 13 years older, so I remember when he was born, and I remember him growing up," Kate said. "Now, we have so much more in common."

"He grew up and got involved in his activities, and I had mine as a young adult, so we saw less of each other," Kate said.

Jude attended and graduated from Kansas State University (KSU), which is Kate's alma mater. When Kate's younger brother Wyatt came to KSU for a campus visit as a senior in high school, Jude joined them. He was a sophomore.

"I realized then how much he had grown up," Kate said. "He was a college student, the time of life when most people are sowing their wild oats, but Jude already had it figured out. Some people have to figure it out through trial and error, but he always knows what the right thing is without having to think about it or make mistakes to figure it out. He never had to be wrong."

She continued: "His moral compass always points true north."

At this point, I can feel my heart swelling with pride, but I am getting a little teary, too. I know my son is a fine young man, but to hear someone else describe him like this makes me wonder where it came from.

"He is the perfect combination of you and Mark (my husband). He is the most evolved human being I have ever known. He has Mark's level headedness, and your sense of adventure. He's straightforward like Mark, yet dynamic, just like you," Kate said.

I continue to swell with pride, but still feel the tears welling, too. I do sometimes wonder how he evolved to where he is now from my best, but imperfect efforts as his mother.

Where he is now, is on the other side of the world. When he and Kate connected again, he was preparing to spend several years in Asia in an effort to improve humanity and give all he can to make this world a better place for everyone.

As Kate and I write this, we are enjoying Thanksgiving weekend 2022 at her mother's house, it is our annual weekend celebration. Kate is now married and has her 16-month-old-son in tow, and now knows that the children we are given come through us and not from us, pre-packaged with their own spirit, their own uniqueness, their own potential and perhaps even their own destiny.

"I just know this is what I want to do," Jude told Kate.

"He is a very inspiring person," Kate said. "I want to be like him when I grow up."

Kate is my 39-year-old-niece, and Jude is my 25-year-old son. I am 56 years old at the time of this writing.

I want to be like both of them when I grow up.

11/19: BECKY

When my children were younger, I worked part-time as a speech therapist, and part-time with a home-based business. This particular business attracted other young mothers with children, which granted me the opportunity to meet many wonderful women.

One of these wonderful women was Becky. She signed up for a gift certificate I gave away, and because I was the boss and the sole employee, I let myself hand-pick the winner. Becky won. I told her the hard truth after she won; I wanted her to know I bent the rules just for her in order to get to know her. She was flattered. Even though technically it was *the wrong thing*, I know I did *the right thing* by choosing her. Hey, I *was* the boss, after all.

We stayed in touch and had even more opportunity to do so when Kristie (October 26th) moved in next door to her. Becky and Kristie became fast friends; we made it a priority for the three of us to get together until Becky's husband was transferred to Kansas City. Life would go on to prove to each of us that in spite of all it has to dish out, friends like Kristie and Becky are meant to be keepers. Becky didn't keep her husband long after that; she knew she had to move on without him for her and her boys.

She is in the Boys Club with Kristie and me, like so many of my lunch dates. Her boys are my younger son's age and five months apart in age, because after one adoptive family chose her and her husband to take their child, another one wanted them as well. They gladly welcomed both boys into their home and their hearts.

We meet in the foyer of *Mimi's Restaurant* in Overland Park, Kansas. I am wearing a blue and brown tie-dye shirt; Becky laughs even before she hugs me because she almost wore hers just like it. We haven't seen each other in over five years, but time and its trials fall away easily. I knew they would, but still, I had a small concern about that.

Becky and her husband sent me a card and a memorial donation after my parents died. It arrived just after I had given everything I had writing thank-you notes to the multitude of thoughtful people who did the same. I didn't even acknowledge it. Shortly after that, she and her husband divorced. I didn't acknowledge that either. I knew she wouldn't hold either of these insensitivities against me, but I never felt good about how I handled them with her.

It doesn't take long for that concern to melt away. We settle into a corner booth, and the smiles and laughter flow. She tells me today that, just as my writing is my salve, she, too, has been writing. Her ability with words lies in writing songs and poetry, and she shares some of those lyrics with me. Her insight is profound and reading between these lines reveals the depth of her charismatic personality. I am speechless at her talent. This is a disturbing thing for me, because it is my job as a speech therapist *and* a writer to be in command of the right words at the right time. She's got me, hands-down.

I continue to be speechless—slack-jawed even— as she continues to tell me of just how far she has come since I last spoke to her. I shouldn't have been surprised, knowing her. Her husband fell down and never picked himself up, even with her help. She filed for divorce on a Friday the 13th, took back her maiden name, highlighted her hair, got Botox treatments, and calls it all "liberating."

"What he did doesn't define me," she said. Her smile is electric, lighting up this dark corner booth.

She recently took a trip to Mexico without her children, where she went diving and four-wheeling. She took up running and races compet-itively and is dating again. In her spare time, she works full-time as a home-care registered nurse for a disabled adult.

I have several addictions, and some are healthy; some are not. Too much coffee, for example. Many of you will understand that one. Only a select few of you will understand this one: I am a junkie for a good pen. One that writes as smooth as butter and feels as if it was made just for my hand. In the days when Becky was married, *and* it was still legal to give them away, her pharmaceutical rep husband frequently gave me a good pen fix. The best one was in honor of my 40th birthday. Several days past, I came home after an awful day. It quickly turned around when I found the box from Becky in the mail. Inside it were 40 premi-um pens, courtesy of Becky and her husband. I thought I'd died and gone to Pen Heaven. She loves that story. I called her "write" away, while trying each of them out on crisp, white paper. She likes to tell the story of how I made noises a married woman shouldn't make without her husband present (*my* husband, that is, not hers). I think of her every time I pick one of them up, and that is *often*.

As with any friend who deserves the most honorable words—and most everyone in this book does—her story took me a long time to write. Today is Tuesday, February 07, 2012, almost three months after our date. I must confess that I slacked on her again and did not get a Happy Birthday shout out to her on February 3rd, just four days ago. I knew it was coming, but I failed to recognize it. I think of her every Super Bowl Sunday, as I did just two days ago. When she lived in my small city, her birthday fell on Super Bowl Sunday one year. She related the story to me of her husband pumping up their sons with this morning greeting upon their rising: "Boys, guess what today is? It's *Super Bowl Sunday!*" There would be no awareness on his part of her birthday until later that week. One of the last few straws on the proverbial camel's back would arrive several years later when, shortly after midnight on her birthday, she was summoned to get her husband out of a bit of legal trouble. This involved the divulgence of her birthdate before he was released to her. The officer kindly offered her a "Happy Birthday." Now, this from me.

One of my goals while completing this project was to stay better connected with these friends. Obviously, I failed to acknowledge this sweet-bitter day for her, and I am trying to think of a way to make it up to her. If she wasn't six inches taller than me, I might offer another of my prized tie-dyed shirts. If I still had my home-based business, I'd offer her another gift certificate. Perhaps I will call her and tell her how much she has inspired me with her strength and offer the perfect words that I am expected to deliver as a speech therapist and writer: Happy Belated Birthday and *Thank You.*

BECKY'S LUNCH DATE—As written by Becky

Why do we need prompting to connect with those we love the most? As time goes by and some miles separate us, I was reminded by Kathleen how much I missed some very dear friends. I wish I could set out on her journey, connecting with 52 friends for lunch dates. I'm officially adding this to my bucket list.

My lunch date was long-distance. I haven't seen Allyson since 2005. We were neighbors in a previous town; she was a mother with a little more experience—a mom of three boys, a club I longed to join. Allyson was my mentor—as a mom, as a friend and as a wife. She taught me social graces and always modeled her faith in our Lord Jesus being most important. We were running buddies. The level of commitment at 5:45 a.m. is exponential when you have someone waiting by your garage door. We borrowed clothes, beaded, and helped each other as friends do without batting an eye.

A promotion for her husband moved my dear friend and her family 10 hours away. This was my first significant loss of a friend I relied on daily. She wasn't my "I need a cup of sugar" friend; she was my "meet me on my steps and pray with me" friend. Have you ever lost a running buddy? If so, you understand.

I knew I couldn't orchestrate a lunch. I'm now a working single mom, unable to jump on a plane and "do lunch." I decided to send Allyson a Starbuck's gift card; we emailed, planned to block out time to be still and enjoy a cup of coffee together, uninterrupted. It was such a happy afternoon. I thought, "Why don't we do this weekly?" "Why don't we slow down and connect with those who mean the most?"

And that's why I love Kathleen—because we think alike, but she thought of this first. I am grateful for her project which, as a result, has awoken me to God nudging my heart. I cannot say I've reconnected with a friend from the past every week, but I do keep a list on my desk of dear ones who need to hear from me. And the connection is often more fulfilling to me than to the friend I intended to surprise and lift me up…paying it forward unintentionally, yet with sincerity and grace.

11/20: TRACY

"We're the Three Musketeers with the feathers in our ears…" Tracy sings with us. "I'm one," she says, "I'm two," I sing, holding up two fingers to her one, and Shari (April 7th) finishes with three fingers: "I'm three!" We show our fingers with a big smile, followed by an even bigger laugh. We still sing this just about every time we get together.

We've been getting together for 40 years now. We started kindergarten together, finished high school together, at which point Shari went a separate geographic way, east to Kansas State University, and Tracy and I went west to Fort Hays State University. We have parted ways since then in the physical sense, but deep down we are three 45-year-old women who maintain a lifelong friendship. Except for Tracy—today she turns 46, and we are celebrating.

I am enjoying my annual pilgrimage to Kansas City to see Tracy for her birthday. I am blessed to be married to a wonderful man (Mark, April 22nd) who realizes the need for a woman like me to get away and spend time with her dear friends. Remember, if Mama ain't happy… (August 8th). He waves me out the door, and my three boys batch it for the weekend. Shari and I celebrate each year in Manhattan; Kansas City beckons me for Tracy's big day.

We spend Saturday evening reminiscing with dear old friends, including Shari (April 7th), Tracy's brother, and two other long-time friends join us to ring in Tracy's birthday—except none of us can stay up until midnight anymore, so we call it a night around 10:00. Since Tracy is hosting her brother at her home, I stay with Shari and meet up with Tracy for lunch Sunday, on her actual birthday. Just like Shari, Tracy now lives in the Kansas City area.

We dine today at J. Alexander's, but I am doing more dining than she is. She has already been treated to one birthday lunch with her brother and sister—she lives in Kansas City, too—so she partakes only of dessert. The waiter brings her a generous slice of carrot cake with a lit candle, and he and I summon our singing talents (I have essentially none) in order to wish her the *Happy Birthday* she deserves.

She deserves so much more than she gets from me, and not just in the singing department. Tracy has been with me in laughter and in tears, and we have both had enough tears, thank you. Her oldest sister—she had three sisters and has two brothers—passed away suddenly almost two years ago; the anniversary of her death is the day after my parents' deaths. We'd both like to wipe the month of March off the calendar. Since we can't do that, we focus on the positive. Tracy was on the phone within minutes of hearing about my parents and hasn't left my side since. I can only hope I have offered her a small measure of the peace she has brought to me throughout the last (almost) four years. Life does go on, but death goes on, too.

Today, however, we focus on life. Her life is rich with family and friends, and today she is celebrated by both. Tracy's younger sister, Tammy, lives close to her in Kansas City, and Tracy is adored by Tammy's three children. Tracy is single and has no children, but she fills a role with those three children that nobody else can. They fondly call her "T.T.", which is a variation of "aunt" in Spanish, even though they speak English. Tammy is a single mother, and Tracy is there for all four of them. None of them would have it any other way.

Tracy works for a medical supply company, traveling through both Kansas and Missouri. She has a heart that senses the needs of her clients, and she fills those needs as much as her job capacity will allow her, and then some. The line between the personal and professional aspects of her job is sometimes blurred, as evidenced by the company she kept just four days after our date: on Thanksgiving, she and her sister in Kansas City celebrated with each other *and* with a client of Tracy's who would have otherwise been alone for the holiday. This client has physical limitations that may have kept a lesser person from attempting to work around these mobility issues, but Tracy and her sister helped her in and out and up and down and gave her the help she needed with personal care throughout the day.

I am mobile, healthy, and ever so grateful. Sometimes, however, I have needs that aren't so obvious. Sometimes I need help getting up, getting myself back together, and I have other personal issues. Tracy is there to take care of all of them. She has been there as long as I can remember, and she will be there in the future as long as both of us have working minds, memories and bodies.

If I only had two friends to call upon for lunch instead of 52, the other two Musketeers would suffice. Lucky for them they don't have to be everything to me, and there are plenty of others to carry the weight when I become heavy sometimes.

The ending phrase in our Musketeers song can't be denied: "Whenever there is trouble, we are never double…I'm one, I'm two, I'm three!" Of course, we all have our fingers up again.

TRACY'S LUNCH DATE

There are very few people who can keep a former flame as a friend, and *their* family and friends, too. There are even fewer who can pull off a tasteful prank at a funeral. Then, there are but a handful who can do both. Tracy is one in that handful.

Tracy had a long-standing relationship with Mark, who brought with him a delightful family and a host of friends. His friend, Jerene, was a delightful woman who, while she was several decades older than Tracy, became Tracy's dear friend. When I challenged Tracy to reach out to someone she needed to make contact with, she knew it was Jerene. She was struggling with health issues and had a grim prognosis. Jerene knew her earthly stay was limited, and so did Tracy. They both knew the value of time, and that it was likely running out for Jerene.

Tracy and Jerene had a delightful lunch date. They dined, laughed, and spoke of old times, but both knew that new times may be limited. They were. Jerene passed away not long after their date.

After the funeral, while Jerene's family was visiting with friends and other family members, Tracy made her rounds with the people she knew. It was a small percentage of the guests, as Jerene was widely known in Kansas City, and many people came to pay their tributes.

Tracy then proceeded to walk toward her car but detoured when she saw the limousine waiting for the family. She opened the front door and crawled into the passenger seat.

"Oh, dang it!" she said to the driver, after sitting for a bit. "I am so used to getting in these things, I just automatically crawl in!"

The driver was able to take a joke and laughed along with her, but the joke ended up being on Tracy.

While words cannot do her beauty justice, just know that Tracy has a Jackie Onassis look. She is strikingly beautiful, classy and carries herself well, just like Jackie did. This trifecta fails to escape only a few red-blooded men, and the limousine driver was *not* one of them. He must have felt that he had hit the mother lode, because he wasn't about to let this opportunity go by.

The driver wasn't her type, but he was sure he was. He immediately engaged her in conversation and, in short order, asked her for a date after his driving gig was done.

She got right out of the limousine. I am sure Jerene was laughing from above.

12/26: BRIDGET

Obviously, it has been over a month since my last date, but since I'm the boss here, I let myself slide. Initially, my plan was to be finished by December 1st, 2011, exactly a year after I started. However, because I value my dear friends more than I do keeping a deadline, I granted myself a month of grace, extending the deadline to December 31st, 2011. There was no other way I could have a lunch date with Bridget. She was in Kansas City when I took Tracy to lunch, but we weren't able to connect then.

Bridget is a mother to five children and 17 grandchildren. She is a dear friend from college, returning to the classroom when she was just a bit younger than I am now, and when four of her five children were still at home. She is a school-based speech therapist in western Kansas and provides therapy in her small-town hospital as well. Bridget is 58 years old, unless you believe her birth certificate, which says she turns 59 today. The error remains to be corrected before she applies for her passport soon, because her true birthday is December 27th. Today, we will call it her birthday because she just happens to be in my small city, and I have the pleasure of taking her to lunch.

The first thought on my mind this morning upon rising was this: *"There is no way I can take Bridget to lunch before the end of the year."* The acknowledgement of potential defeat hit hard: she was two-and-one-half hours away, it's the holidays, she has her family and I have mine, it's her birthday, the flu is spreading through my house…and then my phone received a text.

She knew how badly I wanted to see her to make her one of my dates, and her text said this: *Merry Christmas. Made an unexpected trip to Salina last night, I'll be here for a while.* The stars and planets had aligned and brought her almost to my door. The reason for the trip was family-related, and everything turned out well. It was, as my Yiddish-speaking friend, Carol, says, "bashert"—fate.

We dine today at El Atoron (Abigail, May 25th), because she let me choose. Of course, I chose Mexican food. The restaurant has since moved downtown, but the food remains divine.

Bridget and I have always had a flow between us. We reached easily across the age span in college and became fast friends. This was 19 years ago this fall, and despite the long months—sometimes more than 12—that pass between our visits, we always fit into that cliché: we pick up where we left off.

Today is no different. I greet her at the door to my office building: she wanted to see it because her mother attended college here many years ago. Bridget's strong faith drew her to the beautiful chapel downstairs as well. She possesses a quiet but strong Catholic faith, and it encircles her like an aura. Spending any amount of time with her leaves you feeling uplifted; in any interaction she leaves behind a natural sense of peace.

Bridget reached out to me the night before my parents' funeral by phone, and she reached out her hand from the end of the pew as I walked out of the church, with my other hand in my husband's. She made the two-hour trip to honor two people she didn't even know, but more importantly, to support me. I will never forget that.

Bridget's lunch date is sandwiched between Tracy (November 20th) and Matt (December 29th). She knows Tracy from another mutual friend as well as through me, and by chance, Tracy is passing through town today on her way back to Kansas City after spending Christmas with her parents. She stops to see both of us at the end of our lunch date; she and Tracy had already been acquainted through me and another mutual friend as well.

My last date of the 52, just two days after Bridget, is with my stepson. Bridget knows him, too, and has known him longer than I have. Bridget lives in the same small western Kansas town where Matt spent his first 10 years. That small town is 90 miles from our college town. When we were in college, she made that three-hour round trip *every day*. She was obviously committed; first to her family, then to her college endeavor. Her commute was made easier when she carpooled with— who else—Matt's mother. She was attending class there, too.

We talk about issues great and small, and as easily as she talks about the weather, she tells me that *for her own life*, she has determined the meaning of life: Live life in accord with all that is good and true and right in order to get to Heaven. She has maintained this sure knowledge since she was 16, just four years after her father died after a brief illness. She knew, even as a young girl, that she wanted to see him again, and this was the way to ensure that reunion. Her mother remains youthful and energetic at age 83, having moved closer to Bridget after being widowed for a third time.

For Bridget's life on earth, this policy dictates the goodwill and peace she shares with everyone she meets. And I thought I was someone special. Turns out, she treats everyone like this.

The name "Bridget" has always sounded like a beautiful melody to me, even before I met her. If I'd had daughters, there is a chance one of them might have her name. I looked up the meaning of her name. It means "strong" and "virtuous." It didn't say anything about "magnetic" or "adherent," but I'll add those to the definition.

BRIDGET'S LUNCH DATE—written by Bridget:
My Lunch Date with Brandi--May 15, 2012

Brandi is 27, one year younger than my daughter. I'm 59. For the last three years, she has been the school psychologist at the school in which I work. For a youngster, she knows her "stuff" and we had quickly established a good working relationship. She followed on the heels of a much-admired, much-loved school psychologist who passed away after a year-long period of suffering with a brain tumor. Brandi was unfazed by the stories that began, "When Donna was here, we…." She advised parents, staff, and students in a professional manner and with the confidence of a seasoned school psychologist.

As a single mom, she had worked her way through her undergraduate and then a master's program to reach her goal as quickly as she could. After graduation, she married her son's father, and they added a sweet daughter to the family. As life sometimes goes, her marriage crumbled, and she again found herself as a single mom.

Now, her life has taken another turn. She will be getting married in two weeks and will be moving two-and-one-half hours to the east. She has accepted a new job and, after next week, our working relationship will cease. So, I invited her to lunch as a sort of "bridal" luncheon and a farewell to this era. We dined at "Oscar's" an upscale coffee shop in the heart of downtown, small-town, Hoxie, Kansas. Oscar's offers quaint al fresco dining that rivals any big city. Beautiful flower boxes and a serene atmosphere are most inviting. However, because the heat was intense, we chose to sit inside where the atmosphere is every bit as charming. She spoke of the humble wedding she and her fiancé will share and her hopes and dreams for a happy future.

I told her about my college friend, Kathleen, and her unique outlook on life. I told her of our lunch date back in December and Kathleen's hope for a world of friends that "pay forward" lunches. Brandi will be a willing participant.

I am thankful for both of my younger girlfriends who have been blessings along my life's path. God bless you both, Kathleen, and Brandi.

12/29: MATT

Twenty-nine days after my projected completion date, I had lunch with my 52nd lunch date. This date wasn't planned from the beginning; I was afraid he would think I was even crazier than he already knew me to be, and besides that, I didn't know if I would be able to pull it off because he lives nine hours away. In the end, just like our beginning together, it was meant to be.

Matt is my stepson, and he was home for Christmas. He assured me he didn't already think I was crazy, and to prove he liked this whole idea, he held up his end of the deal just 24 hours later. On his way back to Minneapolis, Minnesota, he spent a day in Omaha, where he had just moved from in August. There was a friend there he knew he needed to connect with, and this gave him the incentive.

We dine today at *Moka's*, just like seven other lunch dates. This spot would prove to be the most frequently visited restaurant in all my *52 Lunches*. I dined at more Mexican restaurants than I did at *Moka's*, but it wasn't always the same one.

Matt is 25 years old. He completed college and is now a leasing manager for a national property company. He was employed by the same company in Omaha, and because of his stellar work performance he was offered a promotion to one of their properties in Minneapolis. He moved just after our July visit. Amy (July 13th) and Kelly (January 21st) live there, too, so I am quite excited that we will now have three very good reasons to make the trek.

Matt is single, and he tells me today during our lunch that while he isn't dating anyone right now, he does hope to find the right person someday, but not just yet. He is wise beyond his years; I have watched him mature and make sound decisions throughout his life that reflect more wisdom than his peers might possess. I can only hope that as they grow and mature, his dad's other two sons got their share of that from him, as well.

He is perceptive, too, knowing that my life as a stepmother wasn't always easy. I assure him today—as I have in the past—that if there was ever a period of time, or even a moment when it may have seemed I was resentful of him, it wasn't him, it was the situation. We maintained visits every other weekend throughout his childhood, even though he lived four hours away for most of it. I was never his mother, per se, she was always present in his life, and obviously did a wonderful job doing her part in nurturing him along the road to adulthood. He laughs as he recalls the only incident that made him think that perhaps I was a wicked stepmother, and when he brought it up, I remembered it, too.

He was eight or nine; his brothers weren't born yet. He was visiting during the summer, and we purchased new shoes for him. He and I were preparing to go to an outdoor festival, and I knew it would be muddy. I wouldn't let him wear his new shoes, and he threw a fit. I held fast to my decision, and he fought me the whole way. If that is the only negative memory he has of me, I guess I did okay in my role as stepmother.

If I ever doubt that he doesn't feel good about the stepmother life handed him, I need only to re-read some of the birthday or Mother's Day cards he has given me since he has become an adult. His expressions of gratitude and deep sense of family he feels with us make me realize all the hardships I suffered in this role were well worth the pain. I knew when I signed up for the package deal known as *Mark and Matt* that it wasn't about me; there would be many sacrifices I was agreeing to accept when I said, "*I Do.*" Those sacrifices have become very few and far between, if at all anymore, and the ones I made in the distant and recent past have paid dividends into my personal savings account of positive life experiences. Think of it as interest earned when I *saved* instead of *spent* my wants in order to achieve the goals that were best for us as a blended family. I am now reaping the rewards.

It wasn't always easy, and in my mind, I don't think I saved as much as I should; I think there were times when I really blew it. Matt tells me today he thinks I always had it together, and he always felt loved and welcomed when he spent every other weekend with us throughout his childhood, up until the time he went to college. When he became independent then, he frequently chose to visit us, often bringing his friends along. Apparently, we were *cool*, cool enough to hang out with his guy friends and, occasionally, a girlfriend. His choices in friends were always good, but he always knew when it wasn't right with a girlfriend—which brings us to *his* lunch date.

MATT'S LUNCH DATE

Today is Saint Patrick's Day. My husband and I brought our boys to Hastings, Nebraska, to join Matt for a men's basketball tournament he is playing in. We are enjoying lunch today at *Rivals*, a sports bar and grill. Matt tells me about his lunch date he had on December 30th, just one day after ours.

He met his friend, Kayla, for lunch at Paradise Bakery in Omaha; she was able to meet on short notice, even though she works full-time as a nurse and has a husband and baby—both in tow for this date. Matt and Kayla have known each other since they were children *and* neighbors in a small Nebraska town. Kayla is one year older than Matt and would frequently be called upon to babysit Matt and his younger siblings. As a mother of sons, I know that even one year of age a young girl has on a boy can make a world of difference in responsibility for younger children—especially when they are the boy's siblings. Matt's mother didn't trust him with the two younger children, but she trusted Kayla. I get this.

Matt and Kayla grew up to become good friends—nothing less, nothing more. They kept in contact throughout college, and both ended up in Omaha. Matt subsequently moved on to Minneapolis but remained in touch with Kayla. In her single days, Kayla had a roommate named Lindsay. Matt and Lindsay met about a year ago, and after seeing each other again about a month ago with these mutual friends, they agreed they would like to see a lot more of each other. She is along with Matt this weekend. He picked her up at the airport in Omaha; she flew in from Phoenix where she is a traveling nurse. I saw her profile and pictures on Facebook before this weekend. She is blonde and beautiful, and I was a bit worried about this. I tell all my single male friends that beautiful blondes are typically trouble. Lindsay, however, is the exception. In short order after meeting her, I am smitten with her, too. I think, perhaps, they are a perfect couple—but it is too early to tell.

Because I am the boss of this whole project, and because I am letting myself get away with straying from the original plan as the project progresses, I am adding a third part to Matt's story. Again, I am the boss. *And,* there is no one better to make an exception for than him—on the last lunch date.

Fast forward now to April 23rd, just over a month after our Nebraska trip. Matt is visiting us for the day and leaving tomorrow morning for Phoenix. Here is the reason for this third phase of his story: One week ago today, his boss strolled into his office early on that Monday morning, and within a few minutes Matt was relieved of his job duties. It seems he inherited the Depperschmidt gene that dictates positive and moral ethics in the work setting. As a manager, he made decisions that were the *right* thing to do but didn't make the company as much money as the alternative. He and his superiors had disagreed about these matters before, but he always stuck to his guns. Today, he had no choice. Plus, the word was already out on the street that he was considering other jobs, and just like a romantic breakup, one never wants to be the one dumped upon, so his boss did the dumping.

Those winter nights in Minnesota are cold when you are alone, and his heart was now in warm and sunny Phoenix. He is taking the proverbial *leap of faith*—just as his father and I encouraged him to do—and he is making the move. He will land on his feet after this leap; he always does. He is smart, charming and a valuable employee. He already has two job interviews lined up, and Lindsay awaits him there….

EPILOGUE

April 26th, 2014 was a beautiful day in Omaha, Nebraska: a bride's dream for weather. Matt and Lindsay became engaged on her birthday the previous June—he went all out on the proposal, but you will have to take him to lunch to hear about that. I am now the step-mother-in-law, a new title I relish. It is sheer delight times two.

Matt now works for a national investment company in Phoenix and has climbed a few steps higher on the ladder than when he started. Lindsay works as a nurse at a nationally recognized clinic in Phoenix, and she is studying to become a nurse practitioner. She will graduate in May 2015.

I told his younger brothers that their older brother set the bar *pretty high* when it comes to picking a spouse. May they choose as well as he did.

BONUS DATES

The lunch dates I am adding at the end are now detailed. They are every bit as important as the first 52 dates, but I decided initially to cut the project off after 52. When some of those chose not to complete the Pay-It-Forward plan, I thanked them, blessed them, and found more. They were not asked to complete a pay-it-forward date, but one of them chose to anyway.

**

JACQUE

I went back to college four years after I graduated the first time. I had those four years of life under my belt, four years of earning just a little bit of money and its accompanying freedom, enough money that I decided in those four years I needed a new car. Along with the car came car payments, insurance, and taxes.

It would be difficult, I knew, to maintain my car payments and expenses, as well as living expenses *and* complete graduate school, but I had to do it. It was a scary proposition, but I had to depend on myself. I was a liberated woman, with only myself to take care of.

**

Jacque was the first graduate student from my alma mater to be placed under my supervision—along with my co-worker Christy (March 11th)—to complete her graduate externship. Jacque had car expenses, too, as she had to drive 200 miles round-trip every day. She could have stayed in an apartment provided by the hospital, but she had to be home every night: she was a single mother to five-year-old Macy. She did it every day without asking for exception or exemption and without complaint. She smiled a lot every day. She radiated confidence, even if she wasn't feeling it. She got it. She saw the big picture in this experience, this career, this multi-faceted experience of completing her college degree—six years are necessary in our profession—while maintaining her status as mother, elevating it above all others.

Tonight, as part of Phase Two of this book, Jacque sits across from me at *Gella's Diner,* a favorite eatery/brewery for both of us in Hays, Kansas, where we both completed our degrees. She is a professor at this college now, more than ten years after she was my student. Because of Jacque, my first book, *The Tip of Your Tongue,* is now on the bookshelf at the university bookstore, as well as the text for the introductory students in this program at Fort Hays State University. Because of Jacque, this afternoon I spoke to the undergraduates who are using my book, and I will speak to her graduate students tomorrow morning. I am so honored; I am speechless—not a good thing for a speech therapist. All thanks to Jacque. She took my book and, in her gentle but assertive way, let the right people know about it.

**

There is a wonderful picture of my parents that we used on the back of their funeral program. We took it at a restaurant during a celebration of their 50th wedding anniversary, and it now sits framed in my home. It was taken at this restaurant, at this table. Tonight, out of perhaps 30 tables in this restaurant, Jacque and I were seated here by chance.

Tomorrow morning, I will tell two stories about Jacque to her students. She knows I will do this; it is on the outline I sent her. She doesn't know what they are, but I have assured her they will be appropriate and flattering. The opening story will illustrate one of her many strengths that I feel is essential for students to possess as they progress through this field of study and into our profession. In essence, it is *strength.*

To end my presentation to her students, I will tell another story to illustrate yet another essential quality for our profession: As the weeks and months passed after my parents' deaths, my siblings, my sons, my husband, and his family and closest friends were my rocks, never forgetting I was still suffering. They kept me close in thought and action, never letting me get down too far. There were also a handful of friends who, while not the closest in geography or friendship, continued to reach out to me in those weeks and months, calling just to let me know they were still thinking of me, that they hadn't forgotten my pain.

Jacque was one of those friends. Her calls would come in at what seemed to be the time I needed them most, always lifting me up a bit when I needed a boost. She spoke the right words to make me realize I wasn't forgotten. This strength, as a necessity in our profession as well, paradoxically, is *softness.* In order to be a balanced therapist, I feel, there must be the perfect blend of *strong* and *soft.* Jacque has both.

Perhaps she developed them out of necessity in order to be a rock for her daughter, while still being a gentle mother. Perhaps she always possessed them; I don't know because I didn't know her before. Jacque is now married and has a nine-year-old son. She continues to radiate both *strong* as well as *soft,* even if her life circumstances now don't require her to be quite as strong as she once was. It is her nature; it is who she is.

I used to be her teacher, and in the morning, she will go on to tell her students I still am. She doesn't know she has taught me as well.

**

Tonight, in this very special town that is home to our beloved college, at this memorable restaurant and brewery, sitting at this sentimental table, we'll drink to that.

ROSE

If I'd had a daughter instead of a boy with either of my two, her middle name would have been Rose. I didn't have any daughters, so I didn't get to use her name.

She didn't know that until she read this. I know she is honored, but she doesn't need to be flattered or approved of in any way by others. Rose is her own woman who makes her own way and doesn't care what others think if it is the right thing for her, and if it doesn't hurt anyone else. I have always wanted to be like her when I grow up in that respect. I like to think I am a work in progress, but I will always hold her as the model.

In 1985, when I was struggling—as so many college freshmen do—to decide upon a major, I fell in love with the study of sociology—thanks to Rose. It was the spring semester after that all-important, unforgettable first semester away at college. I needed to get real and make some decisions about the trajectory of my college future. I had no idea what to be when I grew up; my original plan didn't fit anymore, so I was shopping. I took Rose's *Introduction to Sociology* as an elective, and I found my first academic love. I had found no other loves in order to earn an M.R.S. degree—as in Mrs.—which, at the tender age of 18, seemed to be an easy way out. Thank you, God, for sending me down what seemed the hard road at that point.

Having no clue what I would do with this degree, I earned it anyway. I loved the study. It liberated my mind. It opened doors I didn't know existed in my mind. I was smitten. Rose taught this science in such a way that made it an art. She made it easy to put myself in all the other shoes presented, to see through all the other lenses offered. It has turned out to be my most valuable education. I still look through those other glasses; wear those other shoes.

And it has made all the difference.

My friends would ask me what on earth I was going to do with a degree in sociology. I would respond: "I'm going to socialize." And so, I have. It is fitting, then, that Rose is my last official "lunch" date. It wasn't even lunch, and it really wasn't a date. I stopped to visit her in her office around 3:00 one beautiful Tuesday afternoon after I gave a lecture to freshman students in speech language pathology at Fort Hays State University, my alma mater and Rose's long-time employer. My master's degree brought me back, as they were using my book, *The Tip of Your Tongue*, as a text in their class. If not for Rose, I wouldn't have written that book. I wouldn't have been a sociologist, and it is written as one, as well as a speech-language pathologist. Her name is in the acknowledgements at the beginning.

Rose seems taken with this idea of paying it forward, and after I explain it in full to her, the wheels in her mind are spinning out loud.

"I could take…or I could ask…" She kept thinking of who the best date would be. Even though we didn't get to have an actual lunch date—the college is 100 miles from my home, and, at 75 years of youth, Rose is still teaching full-time. She says she is really going to retire this spring—31 years after she taught me as a freshman. So, it was hard enough to find this half-hour that I was on campus and she was free. Not that she wouldn't have been worth a special trip; I should have done that long ago.

But I didn't. And this book is not about dwelling on what could have been, or should have been, it is about what is right now and what could be if we all make the effort to connect.

Today, we did. Rose knew the heartbreak I endured when my parents died; she even got to meet my mother years ago. My mother knew Rose was a special woman to me and, knowing that love multiplies when you share it, Mom was eager to meet this incredible woman who had so positively impacted her daughter. She thought the world of her, too.

My mother also loved the artistry of Mary Engelbreit. Every year I would give her the daily calendar featuring her artwork and quips, and every year Mom would act surprised. She often would enclose one of the pages in a card if it was a favorite and if it fit, or she may send them in the mail just because. In my mother's honor, I now buy the calendar every year, and I give away or send the pages to someone if it fits.

Today's entry, October 18th, 2016, features two acrobats on separate trapeze swings, just about to reach other. Very simply, it says, *"Only Connect."*

Today, Rose and I connected. It was that perfect. It was that simple. And I sent her that calendar page.

ROSE'S DATE--written by Rose

I am grateful to my former student Kathleen for her outstanding performance in the classroom years ago, for living by the principles in which she believes, and for reminding me that life is short and our opportunities to "pay it forward" are limited, so we should embrace them every day.

I "paid it forward" by taking my neighbor, Mitzi, to coffee and dessert. I did not know Mitzi and her husband, Earl, well when they faced the tragedy of their daughter's death. In retrospect, I always felt I could have been more supportive at the time of their loss. I cried when I learned of her death. I clipped the tribute that appeared in the newspaper, and, for reasons unbeknownst to me, I kept that beautiful tribute to Carla in my desk drawer…something I never do.

On my date with Mitzi to "pay it forward," I showed Mitzi the tribute, now yellowed with age, and expressed how beautiful the tribute was and how I wish I had been more supportive. As human beings, we are given shoulders to offer to others to cry on even if the others are not close friends.

Mitzi and I talked and talked. We talked about Carla, who accomplished so much in her short life, who was an artist in her own right as expressed by her needlework creations, and who was a loving daughter. We talked about death, but mostly, we talked about life. I registered my feelings of inadequacy at the time of her loss, and I asked if I might share the tribute written with such love. She agreed.

I shared with Mitzi that the most helpful message given to me when my 21-year-old son-in-law was killed in an automobile wreck came from a friend who said, "BE GLAD FOR THE TIME YOU HAD HIM." Mitzi and her family knew this and wrote in the tribute, "Our great sadness in her death is surpassed only by our gratitude for her life."

Thank you, Kathleen, for teaching your former teacher an important lesson. Our shared humanity can be expressed in a simple act of "paying it forward."

Epilogue: Shortly after I saw Rose in October 2016, she took Mitzi out and sent me this story on November 10th. A few weeks later during the Thanksgiving holiday, Rose's husband suffered a fall in their home and died on Christmas Eve. I wish I could have done something to help ease her pain.

I did get to visit her again almost a year later. She had retired, and I stopped by her home on my way to Colorado, not yet having met up with my sister for the last leg of the trip. She was preparing to move to Denver, Colorado, to be near her daughter, their only child.

She remained positive and upbeat, which is her usual default setting. She simply moved forward, remaining grateful and GLAD FOR THE TIME SHE HAD HIM.

We connected again, and, unbeknownst to her, she continued to teach me.

MARCIA, MARCIA, MARCIA!

Marcia deserves to have her name in print three times, because she offers about three times as much kindness as the average person. Unlike the Marsha who made this line famous—and her sister—Marcia gets it. She is able to step outside of herself and see through someone else's eyes; feel someone else's pain.

When my parents died, we received an unbelievable outpouring of care, support, love, concern and—flowers. Food was another commodity that came in abundance, and I will be forever grateful to all those kind people who gave any show of support, in whatever form it came it—edible or not. Marcia gave me something that only a handful of people gave, something that represented great foresight as well as insight, something that would be healing and nourishing both physically and mentally, as well as something that filled a need: a restaurant gift card.

We had so much good food that kept us fed—body and soul—for about a month. We were able to freeze a lot of it, too, which always is a great ace in the hole when the cupboard is bare. Having a restaurant gift card, however, gave us the opportunity to dine out and enjoy great food, but more important than that, it got us out of the house. It became very easy to be reclusive in the weeks and months after, so we were. We needed to get out, become part of the human group again, but it wasn't easy. The gift card gave us the perfect opportunity to do just that.

Now, when I have any input into what to get a person who has lost a loved one and likely has an abundance of prepared food on hand from so many generous people, I suggest a gift card to a restaurant—thanks to Marcia.

As I write this, it occurs to me that, coincidentally (even though I don't really believe anything is a coincidence), Marcia and I dined at the same restaurant for our date that she gave us the card to: Applebee's.

Marcia and I have more reason now than ever to get together. Not long ago, she lost her mother after an extended illness. As I tell anyone who loses their mother, *"We are never old enough to lose our moms."* There is something about the mother-child relationship that, in most cases, is different from that with the father. The mother is typically the nurturer, and we never stop needing to be nurtured—ever. Marcia's dad remains in the St. Louis area where Marcia grew up.

It is fitting that Marcia and I dine together, not just because she now speaks the language, but for several other reasons, too. We had been saying we needed to do it *forever,* because when we both left the hospital—our shared place of employment—to do our own things, we didn't get the chance to see each other as much.

Marcia's children—a son and a daughter—are a few years older than my boys, and, many years ago, they babysat my children. They, too, live north of our small city and just a few miles east of me, so we were neighbors in the rural sense—sort of. To add to these reasons, eating is an important activity for Marcia: she is a dietician. Thus, the idea of dining together was an idea whose time had come—and gone— a long time ago when we first said: "We should have lunch!" We were finally able to get our "busy" schedules to jive, and we had lunch. And, like every other one of the "Phase Two" lunch dates, she didn't mind a bit.

SHELLY

Finally. Shelly was yet another lunch date that took continued efforts at setting a date, but we finally did it. Shelly is an OT, an Occupational Therapist, who works, just like Andrea and Darcee, as well as Nancy (March 8th), with her heart and her hands. Gina, my friend who passed away was an OT as well. OTs are hard to find to fill any job vacancy, but I seem to have a plethora of them in my life. I am aware of this blessing.

Shelly and I met when we were mutually employed at the lone hospital in our small city. Shelly now works in the public school system with Darcee and moonlights at one of the home health agencies I work at, so we see each other in passing there as well. I thought all this was enough, so I didn't ask her to lunch for the first round. I wish I hadn't stopped at 52 then; she was a casualty of that low number.

Shelly was close to Gina, my friend who inspired me to continue my efforts to bring this project to fruition. She loved and lost her, too, just like so many of us did. By losing her dear friend she, too, knows that life is too short.

Shelly and her husband have two daughters who are about five years younger and the same distance apart in age as my sons. We share motherhood as the most incredible and cherished role in our lives, even though I speak the language of boys, and she speaks in tones of pink.

No matter, we connect on so many levels. We have both kept ourselves free to roam professionally, never hesitating to make changes to maximize our levels of happiness in our jobs. Some people remain in a committed job relationship for years, but not us. Our only long-term commitments are to our families, and to this friendship. It has been around awhile, longer than any professional role either of us has held. She gets me on that level, and so many others.

We meet today at a local favorite in the downtown of our small city. *Martinelli's* is our hometown, homegrown Italian restaurant. Their salads are locally famous, and their pastas—hands down—have so much more personality than some you may find in a franchised restaurant. Not that there is anything wrong with the franchise that fed me with my other OT friends, but this one has its own intimacy and charm that can't be matched for a quiet lunch date like the one we are finally celebrating today.

We have a corner table with partial walls surrounding it that give us the feeling that we have our own little corner to ourselves. We talk easily as we always do, we even commit the crime that your mother told you not to, the crime that OTs and especially speech therapists would scold you for: talking with food in your mouth. We have too little time to share, and too many things to talk about, so we both see no other way. Fortunately, neither of us choked—the cardinal risk in this crime that I preach against.

We talked about our kids, about our work, and about our *ideas.* Shelly has always been a creator of good ideas and is creative in so many other ways. As an OT, she knows not to take the functioning of her hands for granted, so she used them in the past to make jewelry. She knew I needed what she had, and although it has been years, I still have a few of her creations.

The ideas she talks about today have an eye toward the future; she is always good at finding new angles to look at old situations and come up with new solutions. She gives me good ideas, too, and we talk about what our futures may hold. No matter what transpires, both of us are anchored here in this small city, and we will, in some form, continue this pattern of interaction both professionally and personally.

Shelly was closer to Gina than anyone else in this book. It was Shelly who contacted me on Thanksgiving morning to let me know Gina had passed. We cried separately then and celebrated her life together five days later at her funeral. Anyone who knew Gina couldn't walk away after her service and return to their life without being touched and ultimately changed for the better. Gina had that power on earth, and especially after her passing.

To dear friends departed and still with us, I thank them for making me a better person.

Again, thank you Gina.

And, to my friend Shelly, *thank you.*

TANYA

Now, when I tell someone I would like to go to lunch with them, I mean it, I plan it and I carry it through. I no longer say it casually. It is easier to follow through right away than try to tackle all those *maybe someday* lunch dates in one year.

When I started this project, Tanya (pronounced like Tonya) was a friend, but not a close friend. She was not yet in the club; now she is. Her father passed away about 10 years ago, and her mother passed away just over one year ago. She is an adult orphan like me, but unlike me, she has no siblings. I have made her an honorary adoptee into my family, especially with my sisters. I can't imagine life without my sisters, and I can't imagine not having sisters. Tanya had a brother who has passed. She did marry into a close family, which is now *her* family.

Her mother spent some of her last days at a wonderful local facility known as *Sunflower Day Center,* an adult care facility which gives caregivers respite during the daytime hours and allows their loved ones to remain living at home. I had heard wonderful things about his place, and only recently did I have the opportunity to see it up close as I had a patient who spends her days there.

"My daughter's name is Tanya," this dear patient of mine said, as she told me about her family. *"Spelled with an 'a'."* She pronounced it as "Tonya," just like my dear friend pronounces her name, just like she spells her name—the name her mother gave her when she adopted her at birth.

Tanya has four children, the youngest two are thirteen-year-old twins—a boy and a girl. Her two older children have given her two dear grandchildren—one each from her older son and older daughter.

I met Tanya when she was the organizer extraordinaire at the same nursing home Theresa (October 12th) works at. She was hired to make sense out of the paper and the people who created it in our therapy department. She kept us on track, kept us ticking; kept our ducks in a row. She is good at that sort of thing. She now does the same thing for a therapy company that planted their home office in my former office building. I gave up my spot there just over a year ago today, and for lunch I brought *Gourmet to Go* just like I did with Christina (August

18th) in my office. Theirs is now down the hall from my former office; I told them there was a great spot open when they were looking for office space, and they took it. I now have a cozy space in my home—I am sitting in it as I write—that serves as my office. My hands-on work is now done in people's homes, offices and one small hospital.

If you read my book *The Tip of Your Tongue,* you will see Tanya's name in the acknowledgements. I asked her to be my left brain during the writing process, and she managed it as well as anyone could who agreed to tackle the daunting task of making sense out of the jumbled mess of ideas and words and good writing intentions that floated freely through my right brain, waiting for someone like her to corral them all and whip them into shape. She did, and my book got done. That's the thing about anyone like me who ventures into their right brain in order to create: the left brain, which typically runs the show and keeps things in order, is abandoned in favor of the right, which floats and flits freely through the meadows of words and ideas inside a writer's right brain. It doesn't like deadlines or ultimatums, which I had given it plenty of times before. It needed someone like Tanya. So, I thanked her in print—except that I spelled her name *Tonya.* Forever in print, it will be spelled wrong, which deeply troubles the expert speller in me.

But not her. She saves her concerns for the big stuff, the stuff that matters. She focuses on things that bring happiness and joy. Both of us, now having lost the two people we loved from day one, are gone. We know the importance of taking life in stride and savoring each day. We both try hard to sweat only the big stuff, if that. Through the time we have spent together, as well as many great phone conversations since our respective initiations into this club, we have tried to pare away the trivial matters, the crap that used to drag us down, and try now to focus instead on anything that brings us up. We have earned it, we deserve it, and we would like to share it with anyone who might want a piece of this delicious pie. There's plenty to go around.

TRACINE

When I was about ten or eleven, my parents loaded all seven of their children into our wood-paneled station wagon on a Sunday afternoon, and we made an epic trip to Abilene, Kansas. We lived on our farm two hours away, and by virtue of the fact that we traveled two hours, I knew this was *a big deal.*

Our destination was the Eisenhower Museum. I had no idea that, almost forty years later, it would still be a big deal to me. Now, today, on this election day, I am having lunch in Abilene with Tracine at Ike's Place, a local favorite bar/grill that celebrates our former president. Dwight David "Ike" Eisenhower, our country's 34th president, grew up right here in Abilene and is buried here, too. The Eisenhower Museum showcases the military and presidential achievements of the man who led the Allied Forces to victory over Hitler in World War II, and then was voted our country's commander-in-chief. He was a pivotal player in stabilizing and enhancing our country's freedom over 70 years ago.

I started this project on December 1st, 2010. I proclaimed this date as my personal Independence Day, as I was launching my new business in my new office that day as well. Now, almost four years later, I realize every day is my Independence Day. As an independent contractor, my work has taken me out of that office and into several contractual positions, as well as private therapy, and a few professional writing projects as well. One of those positions is at the hospital here in Abilene, exactly 30 minutes from my garage. I served this small-town facility ten years ago and left to take a full-time position closer to home. I never lost the feeling of home I felt when I was there. Nine months ago yesterday, I went back. It only took me one day to decide after they invited me back. It was liberating. I like Abilene, and *I like Ike.*

Thanks to the sacrifices of so many amazing men and women, I *am* liberated. I am free to do my own thing, free to vote in my local/state mid-term election today, free to choose my path, free to earn my own money and spend it at Tracine's.

Treasures by Tracine beckoned me many years ago—nine or ten, perhaps. Her small boutique in downtown Abilene showcases her unique works of art that I and so many other women choose to adorn our bodies with. She is a jewelry maker extraordinaire, an artist in the truest sense. You cannot find these pieces anywhere else. Her marriage of stones and beads allows her to form necklaces, bracelets, and earrings into one-of-a-kind treasures.

Of course, she liked me; I spent a lot of money there. But that reason faded in time. Tracine has a quiet creative energy that drew me to her, made me want to create my masterpiece(s), just as she did. She was doing it, and she wasn't looking back. I wanted to be like her when I grew up, even though I am a few years older than her. She let me inside that sphere of warmth and creativity. I needed her inspiration. We became friends. I am so lucky.

Tracine is a native Abilene girl, having grown up here with her two brothers. Her parents are youthful and active, and her mother works with her at her store. She is married to Oral, an environmental engineer who recently completed his PhD degree through Kansas State University. Completing this degree required that they temporarily relocate to Indiana. Not as much as her mother, I am sure, but to a degree—selfishly—I worried she may not come back home to her family, her town, her store. Her mother and I needn't worry. She is home.

Like a moth to a flame, I frequently find myself in her store now that I travel to Abilene nearly every day. Sometimes I feel the need for a fix, a little piece of her creativity that will sate my desire—for a while. Sometimes I say I just want to come in to say hi, but usually I am drawn in by the temptation. The Treasures start whispering to me when I enter, and, before long, their drone is too much for me to resist, and I find myself at the cash register. After a few of these visits I realized she needed to be part of this book, so I invited her. She didn't refuse.

Seventy-nine months ago today, my parents went to Heaven. This project would not be in existence without the wisdom, strength, and peace I have gained since then.

Tomorrow, my senior-in-high-school son will come to the Eisenhower Museum on a field trip. I have taken both sons there several times to show them how lucky we are to have this Treasure in our backyard, geographically speaking. I had to travel two hours to get here when I was their age. Most visitors have to travel much further than that.

One week from today, I will observe Veterans Day. I make a point to thank any veteran or active-duty military member, and I wear some form of red, white, and blue. I give thanks for my national liberty more than I do on a typical day.

Eight months from today I will once again celebrate our country's Independence. Every day until then—and on that day as well—I will celebrate my own. Thanks in part to Ike Eisenhower, I live in a free country. Thanks in part to Tracine, I can express that freedom in any way I choose, including the jewelry I wear.

Happy Fourth of November to you. May every day be your personal Independence Day, too.

DEANNA

Sometimes friendships happen by association, sometimes by geography, sometimes through school and sometimes because of tragedy. Sometimes, it is all these together. That's how Deanna became my friend.

Deanna is mother to two of my youngest son's classmates: a boy and his twin sister. They live a few miles east of us in the country, along the county line road that places both of us in *Ottawa County*. I have always been drawn to her warm spirit, her beautiful smile, and her easy manner. I would be remiss if I didn't tell you she has a great laugh, too.

Her laughter and smiles were taken away for a while just like mine were. She has them back now, but she knows they are hard-earned.

Deanna lost her father suddenly a few years ago. Her mother died on Christmas morning not yet a year ago. She has three older brothers and no sisters. She remains close to her brothers.

She is in the club. Like me, she is an island. One of the best descriptions of what it feels like to be without one's parents is this: the parents were the continent, and the children are islands. The continent has sunk, but the islands remain, and they are still connected to each other, just not to the mainland—on land anyway. The connection remains, but it's not the same without them on Earth. I hope you don't know the feeling I am talking about.

Deanna is a hairdresser extraordinaire, owning her own shop. When imminent domain threatened the shop she worked in, the shop she was *going* to buy, the deal didn't work out. She found better digs, and now she is the boss, the queen of her new and improved shop. Something tells me she doesn't act queenly over her stylists, because that's not her style. She is a vibrant, dynamic, and beautiful woman, but she doesn't fully realize all that, so how could she lord it over anyone if she doesn't know that about herself? That, and mostly because despite this beauty, this energy, this incredible sense of personal style, she is humble, kind, and warm to others.

This humility allowed her to be flattered, rather than insulted when I asked if she would like to be included in the book as part of Phase

Two. She wasn't insulted to not be a part of the first round; she understands that we grew closer with our shared losses. So, she will fit right into a spot that was vacated, and I am happy to continue to pay it forward for someone else with her as my lunch date.

We met at an authentic Mexican restaurant—again, it's Mexican food. I think it was her idea, and I am always up for it. The meal itself, as well as the restaurant, matter little; it matters that we finally made it happen, just like we said we would.

ANITA

"...And I'm proud to be an American, where at least I know I'm free. And I won't forget the men who died who gave that right to me."

Those men didn't have a face to me, and they didn't have mothers. They do now. The soldier's face in the picture was bright with a warm smile, and his mother's name is Anita. She has been my friend since our days of mutual employment at the hospital in my small city. I was drawn to her quiet energy and warm spirit; she welcomed me as a friend. I left there over six years ago; she left eight years ago. We didn't stay close enough.

Her son, Sergeant Evan Seam Parker, died on October 26th, 2005, at Landstuhl Army Regional Medical Center in Landstuhl, Germany, at the age of 25, leaving behind two young sons. He was serving in *Operation Iraqi Freedom* when a piece of shrapnel from an improvised explosive device (IED) tore through his brain on October 23rd, 2006, by a roadside ambush attack. He was life-watched to Germany, to this, the largest United States Army Hospital outside of the U.S., and his family was told to come immediately. They would keep him alive until his mother, father and older brother arrived.

Anita is a respiratory therapist (RRT) who is now employed at a large hospital in Wichita. I hadn't seen her since shortly after my parents died. My friend Shelly (April 11th) took the day off for me to do whatever I wanted, just six weeks after my life hit the wall. We met Anita for lunch in Wichita. It had been too long then, and too long now. She understands today that she will be part of my *52 Lunches* book but was obviously not on my first list of 52 lunch dates. She didn't care. She's not petty.

Anita's work as an RRT involves therapy to provide oxygen and bronchial therapy to those in need, maintaining artificial airways and management of chronic lung diseases. Her job also requires that, with a doctor's order, she removes the oxygen when it has been decided that the patient's lung function with the respirator is the only thing keeping them alive when the other vital organs have shut down. When the medical staff and the family agree, she carries out the order. She has done it many times.

Anita arrived in Germany in order to see her son one last time. He was kept alive by a ventilator. He had begun "posturing", which is when the limbs begin to stiffen and turn outward. This is expected with severe head trauma. She had seen it many times before.

When she saw her son, she knew it was to say *goodbye*. All three of her sons, she tells me today, loved to play with their ears as children. Even as adults, they would frequently tug on their ears for comfort. Anita caressed Evan's left ear as she spoke lovingly to him, telling him *"It's okay, you can go. I am here."* Evan turned his head to the left, cradled her hand and face, as if to say: *"Mom, I waited for you. I am glad you are here."*

"I have never seen that before." The attending doctor said. "That's not posturing."

"That's not for you." Anita said to the doctor. "That is for me."

Anita was given the opportunity to be the one to let him go. Just like with so many of her patients, she could be the one to make that last move. The ventilator was the same kind she has always worked with, she knew how to do this. She needed a little time and family support before she did, but she did. She saw it as an honor. It was the right thing for her to do.

Most of her patients, she tells me, are able to hang on for at least an hour. Evan was gone within three minutes.

**

With Veterans Day just three days from today, we decide that American food is the most appropriate, and we meet at Red Robin for juicy hamburgers and fries. We talk about life after loss, and how we have both found ourselves in a higher place than we have ever known. We speak of keeping our loved one's legacies and spirits alive, and how we have found places in our hearts that we didn't know existed, depths of love and grace we'd never visited until we had to reach deep down inside and plumb them in order to survive the disabling grief we both experienced at first. We reach out to each other as members in this awful club no one wants to be in, but we both realize that each of us is strong in our own right, and we only need each other to buoy our already strong spirits, not to get through any more darkness that our grief once wrought upon us. We are at peace in this new world, and we want to share it with others who still struggle. We speak of those who are hurting long after their loss, but who won't let us in to help, as well as those we feel we can help. We want to share whatever we can with whoever we can provide comfort. We understand the language spoken in this foreign land of grief. We also speak it. We get it.

Our time with grief is now measured in years, no longer in months. Just as a new baby's age is measured first in weeks, then months and finally years, so, too, is our grief.

Anita speaks of her work over the years with surviving families who have suffered the loss of their Fallen service member. She speaks too of her work with *Operation Freedom* Memorial in Wichita's Veteran's Memorial Park to honor those killed in action in Iraq and Afghanistan and in acts of terrorism. She downplays her role, simply alluding to the fact that she was the driving force behind it. She didn't make it sound like she was the most important player in the game of raising funds, clearing hurdles with the City of Wichita, and pounding the pavement to get support and funding from others. In short, it wouldn't have happened without her. She simply made it sound like she had done a little work to help get it done. At least, that's the impression I left with.

After an afternoon of shopping—possible as one of the many freedoms of an American woman—I met my uncle Don for dinner. Don lives in Wichita, and was married to my mother's sister Jeanne, who passed away in 2005. They had two sons who have both passed too young due to serious illness. I try to get there more often to see him, but just like with Anita, I haven't seen him in far too long.

Don can't see me. He is blind; he has been his entire adult life, as was my aunt Jeanne. Their sons were blind, too. Don is nearly 82 and led an active work life as a manufacturing employee at Beech Aircraft. Don spends much of his time listening to the radio and television, staying abreast of local, regional, national, and international news.

When I told him who I had lunch with, he responded heartily "Oh, yes! I have heard all about her. She is all over the news with her work for the Veteran's Memorial and Gold Star Mothers."

When I got home, I did an online search. I typed in her name, and it showed all the amazing things she has done. She spoke humbly about it all to me, but with quiet pride. I knew it was her mission to support the memory of her son and all our Fallen soldiers, I just didn't know how much work she had done. She is president and founder of the Operation Freedom Memorial Foundation (ofm-ks.com). This was her idea, and six years after the idea came to her while walking through

Wichita's Memorial Park, the memorial was dedicated in May of this year.

Anita promised her son in his last moments that his spirit, his memory, and his name would never be forgotten. Along with many other names, his is etched in beautiful black stone, never to be forgotten in the Operation Freedom Memorial.

**

It is important to distinguish between Memorial Day and Veterans Day, and Anita reminded me of this: Veterans Day is the day to show our gratitude to our veterans, while Memorial Day is the day to honor and remember those who gave the ultimate sacrifice for our country, as well as their families.

**

My father was not a veteran. He escaped the draft thanks to his flat-as-a-pancake feet. Now, all seven of his children have flat feet to a degree, but we might not be here without them. None of my six siblings have served.

My uncle Don was obviously not a veteran with his disability. Jeanne, however, served as a civilian. Her blindness did not stop her from working as a medical transcriptionist at the Veteran's Administration Hospital in Wichita for many years. She didn't need to see; she simply put on the headphones, listened to the doctor's dictation, and typed. She put words on paper to help the Veterans receive the care they needed. She was amazing.

My father-in-law is a Korean War Veteran. My sons, my husband and I wrote him a letter last night, thanking him very personally for his service.

My freedom is not free. I realize this more with each passing Veteran's Day, every 9/11 anniversary, every Independence Day, and to a degree, every day of my life. My national liberty translates into personal liberty for me, and I exercise and appreciate it. I am blessed as an American.

Thank you, Anita, for the gift of your friendship.

Thank you, Sergeant Evan S. Parker, for the gift of my freedom.

"God Bless the USA."

LINDA

Sometimes, ideas hit us on the heat—figuratively, of course. Other times, they really do hit us on the head—literally.

I hadn't seen Linda in 24 years, since I visited her when I lived in Philadelphia. I spent one year there from February 1990 through February 1991 as a nanny for a suburban family. Linda was from Howell, New Jersey—just across the Delaware River and not too far past that.

Before that, I hadn't seen her since 1986, when I spent the fall semester at Eastern New Mexico University (ENMU) in Portales, New Mexico, on the National Student Exchange. Linda wanted a college experience far away from home, and she found it in New Mexico. As a junior, she too participated in the National Student Exchange, spending a year in Maine. She was a freshman at ENMU when I was there as a junior.

I spent a much-needed weekend getaway in Kansas City with Tracy (November 20th) and Shari (April 26th) on this weekend before Thanksgiving 2014, and I let her know via Facebook I would be in town. I wanted to see her again, as we had casually messaged each other about when we first got back in touch last summer. I meant it; this entire project is to show that *I really did mean it when I said we should get together.*

We sat down for an afternoon coffee shop visit in Kansas City. We couldn't make it for lunch, so this was the next best thing. One of the first things I said to her was this: "Linda, I wouldn't have thought to friend you on Facebook. I am so glad you found me."

"I wouldn't have thought of it either, it had been so long, but then something funny happened," she said. "I was in a small closet in my basement where I store holiday decorations and birthday stuff, and a box of old letters fell off the top shelf, hitting me on the head on the way down. The letters spilled on the floor, and I noticed one from you. I remembered you. I knew you were from Kansas, and since I had moved to Kansas City, I thought I'd see if I could find you." I am so glad she did.

The years fell away as the cliché said they would, and we connected once again. Those 24 years brought us each a husband, three kids for her and three for me with my stepson. Her father is in Heaven too; her mother is still in New Jersey. Her Kansas-born husband works for the US government as a Homeland Security Officer; he will be in Ferguson, Missouri later this week when the landmark Grand Jury decision is announced. I hope and pray they don't need his help to keep law and order.

She tells me today that she may not stay married; it has been a challenge on many levels. Our exchange already became emotional when we revealed the loss of our parents; and now her personal struggles become evident. She apologizes for unloading this on me; I assure her that I will do what I can to lighten that weight, even though I have never had to carry it for myself, so I don't truly know how she feels. I reassure her that I know she always was and still is a strong, beautiful, and vibrant woman—on the inside and out—and this strength will carry her and her children through this heartbreak. I wish I could do more. I give her my books on our departure—hopefully, as an avid reader, some of my words on loss will speak to her. I feel helpless otherwise.

That semester at ENMU was a crucible for me; a time that stripped me to my core and rebuilt me over a long period of time in the months after. I struggled with a doomed dating relationship that I tried to extricate myself from, but he wouldn't have it. It became a very real and very scary struggle, and I needed help from every friend I had there in order to leave it all behind and get home safely—and alone. I have apologized to those friends who thought I lost my mind, who wondered how I got in so deep with someone obviously so wrong for me. I am not sure either, except that I was young, scared and far away from home, and when I became friends with the right people, the wolf in sheep's clothing tried to be one of them. I needed all the friends I could make in this new world, so I let him in.

I will forever appreciate all those friends who stood by me, as well as those who were my friends but may not have known how much I struggled. Linda was one of the latter, I didn't reveal this crisis I found myself in then to her until we met again in New Jersey four years later.

Facebook has been a societal blessing as well as a curse. For our friendship, it was a gift. It opened up a fast lane on the expressway for two old friends to catch up with each other, and for that, I am thankful. I don't know that we would have connected again otherwise. I realize our friendship will likely remain casual; time, distance and life circumstances separate us at this point in our lives. That is okay, but I do want to keep in closer touch without letting years go by again.

I hope and pray she finds peace with her situation; I can sense today that she has the inner strength to survive and eventually flourish again. My struggle to leave a relationship didn't involve three children and a marriage, and I know how hard that was. I was able to drive far away and leave it all behind; she can't do that. If we could both participate in another exchange, I would take her pain away and give her my joy; I can make more.

I wish her success in her pursuit of happiness, and joyous freedom, Philadelphia style.

To honor those lifelong friends from that semester at ENMU who couldn't make a lunch date for the book, I want to recognize them in print:

Denise, Sparta, Wisconsin
Diane, Cushing, Maine
Scott, Hemet, California
Carlos, Bogota, Colombia

I wouldn't have made it without you four.

MICHELLE

This seems to be the weekend to remember the days of the National Student Exchange. Yesterday I met Linda in Kansas City after not seeing her for 24 years. My excuse was that we didn't stay close, and I thought she still lived in New Jersey—not exactly a hop, skip, or a jump.

Today, I meet Michelle in Topeka, Kansas on my way home to Salina. There's no excuse for this one: I knew she lived in Topeka (nary a hop, skip *and* a jump), we both grew up in the same small—350 people—town, we went to the same college, we both participated in the National Student Exchange out of that college in the same semester, we even took a road trip to Phoenix, Arizona, checking out my potential exchange college in New Mexico on the way, circa Spring Break 1986.

It had been perhaps eight or ten years since I spoke to her. *No excuse for that.* We were Facebook friends; it doesn't get any easier than that to connect. *But I didn't.*

Michelle and I share several uncanny abilities: remembering dates from long ago, we are both runners, we both write from the heart, to name the most notable. Her online blog is inspiring, and her words speak to the place in me where my words come from—wherever that is. I can't name it, but I feel it. We're both "Tipton girls"; for those of you not from Tipton, this joke purposely goes over your head. (Sorry, I do realize that is most of you, but for those of you who get it, it is priceless. We even discussed the value of that virtue in our lives today; it is a *good* thing.)

Like everyone from Tipton, Michelle knew my parents. Everyone knows everyone else; this is a given. My father was outspoken, everyone knew where he stood, what he believed in, and how he felt about any person, issue, political figure, historical event, color of farm tractor and likely even the weather. My mother, however, was quietly decisive. Her opinions and feelings were hers alone, but some people who could perceive her quiet strength, knew just where she stood. I didn't fully realize this until today, six and three-quarter years after they died.

Michelle made me realize it. She tells me today that when my mother was involved in a school or church event in Tipton, she knew it would come off without a hitch. My mother quietly commandeered the platoon of teenagers she was entrusted with in order to make it happen—whatever event "it" was. She did all this in her own calm, peaceful way, but those select few like Michelle could hear her thoughts: "*It's okay—I've got this under control.*" And it was always *okay*.

In the first raw, bitter days after our parents died, I remember gobbling up any memories or thoughts other people shared about our parents. I—and my siblings too, I know—were so hungry for words that would continue to feed our faith in their incredible legacies. All we had wasn't enough. "*Give me all you've got.*" I remember thinking this as so many kind people shared so many kind words about our parents. Today, the first time I have sat and talked with Michelle since then, I am feeling that raw hunger again. Our big lunch is spread out in front of us, but I am hungrier for her words, her memories to sustain me than my food. Her words about my mother hit the spot, but I will always be hungry for more of them.

Michelle is wife to Scott, who grew up close to our hometown. She is mother to Tanna and Dane. Tanna is a college student who is studying nursing, and Dane is a freshman in high school. We both gave birth twice, both married true gentlemen. We both work in the medical field; Michelle is a trainer for a pharmaceutical company, and travels by land and by air to a multi-state area. She loves gardening, and I love to partake of what my gardener husband grows. She wants to see his garden; she too has built raised boxes in her garden, just as my husband has in ours. I invite her to stop by anytime, I am on the way home to Tipton for her.

If it is possible for 34 years to fall away in just one weekend—24 with Linda yesterday, and I will guess ten with Michelle—then they did. Michelle has that quiet, but direct current of energy that I can connect with, even after a period of years. I quickly realize we are at the same frequency on the FM dial. We have both grown to realize that in spite of our apparent "success"—as defined by society, we crave more than that. Michelle has lost close friends, a loss deep enough to show her that life as we know it is not granted, and neither are those in it whom we love. We both realize that not everything we learned growing up is as magical or as dreadful as we may have once believed, but both of us have structured our lives, our families, our beliefs, and our faith to see just how phenomenally beautiful life can be. And it is.

A BEAUTIFUL DAY IN MY NEIGHBORHOOD

I didn't invite any of my neighbors to lunch. Shame on me. They are, hands down, the most kind, diverse, neighborly, and favorable neighbors a woman could ask for. I didn't ask them to lunch because I see them all the time—or so I thought.

Yes, I would see them in passing, as in *passing by their house and waving, passing them in the driveway and waving, or passing on an invitation to get together*. Those kinds of *in passing* don't count for what I am trying to accomplish here.

So, as an effort to treat them all equally, I invited them all at the same time. I had them all over one Friday night, when, miraculously, none of us had anything else we had to do—except Diane, and she did have something better to do, like celebrate her mother's 85th birthday. So, she did. The rest of us ate enchiladas after we had sipped adult libations, snacked on guacamole, and before we ate cheesecake for dessert. We took over my basement which is normally the guy's domain, but we made it ours for the night.

I had another reason for getting everyone together. Knowing how much it means to have someone attend a funeral for your loved one(s) when they didn't even know them, I had to make it up to Sheila. She didn't know my parents, and yet, she was there for me. When her father passed away recently, I wasn't able to attend the funeral, and none of my neighbors were able to make the hour trip, either. So, we decided to give her a private dinner in honor of her father, and we gathered the girls together to celebrate his life. In her usual humble fashion, she didn't want much attention. Her father passed away after a long and blessed life, and she simply wanted us to remember that. Her mother remains, and they remain close.

Sheila lives just up the hill from me, a stone's throw if you throw it hard enough. She has three children and is living the empty nest lifestyle starting this year, when her youngest child and lifelong friend of my firstborn headed east to Kansas State University—KSU-- for their first year of college last fall. Her oldest child---a daughter-- was married in their beautiful backyard last fall, and the middle child is attending my alma mater: Fort Hays State University, just 100 miles west. Sheila is a nurse in the cardiac rehabilitation unit of our regional hospital in our small city, a fitting job for a woman who cares so well for other's hearts in her kind ways. Her husband is just as neighborly; my husband has known him long before we got married. Good thing he's such a good guy because he is our banker, too.

We live in a rural cul-de-sac, a small loop off the highway with four homes. Down the hill to the south from Sheila lives Angie. Angie and her engineer husband Dan have one daughter, and she, too, is a student at KSU. As a senior, she is making big life decisions, and she has decided to pursue a master's degree in my field: speech-language pathology. I hope and pray I have influenced her in a good way.

Angie is an artist, having held several positions to allow her to express that side of her brain: the right side, the side I hope to keep developing. I take notes from her, but I don't think she knows it. There are many things about Angie that I like, one of them is that she understands my sense of humor. That is not an easy thing for just anyone to do, and she does it well. I can let it all hang out around Angie, and she gives it all back. Laughter is good medicine, and she doles it out generously.

Continuing in clockwise fashion around our neighborhood, first with Sheila, then Angie, and now on to Loretta. Loretta is the newest addition to our neighborhood. While she is out of the loop—the cul-de-sac loop, that is—she is in it in every other way. Loretta and her husband moved to this area from western Kansas, way out west where the Germans once ruled (and some still do), and now have dispersed across the state and the country. My husband's Volga-German family started out in that area of the state, and, given our unforgettable last name, they immediately recognized it when we introduced ourselves. We were in. They knew we were their kind, and I am so glad we are. They are parents to three grown children and three grandchildren. Loretta is the kind of friend who would give you the shirt off her back, or perhaps a kidney if you needed one. However, she no longer has one to spare, because she gave it to her grandson to save his life. Otherwise, I have no doubt she would give it up if any of us needed it. She is just that kind of person. Her grandson, most of all, is so lucky to have her in his life. So are we.

Crossing the highway and walking a short jaunt north, we arrive at Sue's house. Sue is my walking buddy; we drag each other out at unpredictable times when either one of us feels the need. We simply call, and if it works, we meet in the middle. We walk and talk, solve the world's problems, relish our future grandmother statuses, talk about how life moves too fast, and most of all, we try to remember how really good life is.

Sue has one child, her son Matt. He lives three hours east in Kansas City and will soon make her a grandmother. Her long-term love, Rick, lives with her and takes good care of her, not that she needs it. Like me, she is her own woman with her own life, but we do appreciate those men in our lives. Hers is handy just like mine, and to illustrate that point, and to show you who she is when no one is looking, she met Rick when they both volunteered to build a Habitat for Humanity home in our small city.

Sue is out of the geographic loop on our side of the road, but she is in another very important loop: She is the manager of the city department that issues commercial building permits. She sometimes taunts me, knowing I love to shop: *"We are getting several new stores in town that I know you will like, but I can't tell you what they are yet."* Thanks, Sue.

Always, though, the wait for the store is worth it. I didn't meet Sue until about 8 years ago, after she had lived there for some time. She, too, was worth the wait.

When Carolyn (January 28th) moved to town, her house was sold to Chris and her husband Kerry. If there could be a suitable replacement for Carolyn, it would be Chris. While Carolyn left some big shoes to fill, Chris is filling them as capably as anyone could—not that anyone could ever replace Carolyn.

Chris and her husband have three grown children, and eight grandchildren. I haven't taken enough time to be the neighbor I should be to Chris, so I can't say I know her well. I do know, however, that whenever I am around her, her laugh infects me, and I end up leaving her presence feeling much lighter for it. So, I really don't have a good reason for not spending more time with her. Perhaps it is that dreaded word—ugh, busy—that keeps us on our own sides of the road, plus she works in a dental office, and values her time to herself like I do. Sue and Chris met years ago in another dental office where they both worked. Sue talked a reticent Chris into looking at the house for sale next door to her. Chris and her husband were looking for a home in the country, and it was love at first sight.

I was fortunate enough to help her celebrate her 60th birthday. Sue, Chris and I took a trip to Wichita to hear one of our favorite female musicians sing to us as we sat in the second row of a small, beautiful theater in downtown Wichita: Mary Chapin Carpenter. We took her music in after we took in a wonderful dinner. We shopped, dined and enjoyed the music in that order, but throughout all the evening's activities, we talked and laughed. We even had a passenger along who needed a ride to Wichita to meet her husband: Anita (March 29th). As small as our small city is, Anita and Chris already knew each other, too. Clearly, Chris fits into the neighborhood, our circle of friends, and into this book as well.

Heading just a half mile north, and up a small hill off the highway to the west lives Bianca. Not only is her name beautiful and unique, so is she. Bianca is mother to Sean, who is my youngest son's friend. Their family moved here from Chicago when Sean was in fifth grade; they had relatives here and heard it was the perfect place to escape the city and raise their son. For them, she tells me, it has been.

Bianca has been a counselor, which explains why she gets it. She understands me with all my flaws--that she knows of—and seems to see the big picture with others as well. She has taken some necessary time off to recover from breast cancer and has maintained her positive state of mind all the while.

Because Bianca is such a unique and beautiful name, I decided to look up the meaning. One description of anyone who has this name included these qualities: kind, sociable and diplomatic. I cannot agree more.

Traveling due west a few miles from Bianca's house, then a few more north on the gravel roads, lives Sonja. Sonja, my longest acquaintance of all these amazing women. Sonja and I remembered our single days together and celebrated our independence in grand fashion. We reveled in our youthfulness, our single-ness, our ability to stay up a lot later than we do now. Sonja and my husband have known each other longer than she and I have. They ran in the same circles, played on the same softball leagues, celebrated life together as friends in search of that special one. She found hers before I found mine and got started reproducing before I did. She makes it look so easy, what with her five children, and I sometimes stretch to pull it all together as a mother of two. I know it's not, she has had her own struggles, but continues to offer her laughter and smiles. We focus on this wonderful present that we find ourselves in now, surrounded by our worth-the-wait husbands, our children—two of her four sons are the same age as, as well as friends of my sons-- and our lives in the beautiful countryside, only a handful of miles from each other. Who would have though this, in that lifetime ago before husbands, children, and life in the country, that we would one day live so close, send our kids to the same school, and have boys the same age.

Sonja was there too, that dark day when friends from near and far who may have known my parents—or maybe not—gathered to support us. She didn't know them; she did know one of my brothers before she knew me, and she came along with Sheila and her husband. I will never forget that she remembered. She had already been there, and I wasn't there when her father passed away. I didn't know, but I know now how important it is.

The circle is now full and has come back around to my next-door neighbor Diane, who could not be here tonight. Remember, she had something very important to do: celebrate her mother's big birthday. That was where she needed to be. When she is home, she is a gift to the neighborhood. Her easy manner, her friendly ways, her laugh and smile make the sunshine in our neighborhood every day, even when it's cloudy. She has three grown children who have given her grandchildren, and another son who passed far too young. Diane speaks the language of loss, knowing full well my pain because her son was taken that way, too. Diane and her husband Skip knew my parents, and they were there to help us mourn, and to celebrate their lives at the funeral.

My memory wanes as I age, I can tell already. But I will *never* forget that so many people who cared about me were there to support me. I will *never* hesitate to go to the funeral of a dear friend's parent if I can. If I can't, I might just invite the girls over again for a night to honor them.

Sheila, this was the best I could do, even though you wanted nothing. I hope and pray I honored your father with our celebration tonight. I didn't know him, but that didn't matter. You didn't really know my parents either, and you were there. You are still here, I know that anytime I need any help small or large from you, you will be there.

Thank you.

In memory of Harry Lewerenz

FINAL THOUGHTS

Oh my. What was I thinking? And why was I thinking it?

I remember clear as crystal when the idea hit me: I was running, my mind was flowing, my spirit was soaring, and my body was springing forward. I can recall exactly how I felt at that moment, the moment this idea was conceived. I felt brilliant and shiny, full of vigor and vim, ready to conquer my world and the 52 neglected friendships/relationships in it. The idea felt brilliant and shiny too, and I couldn't figure out why no one else had ever done this—at least that I knew of.

Now I know.

I was innocently naïve. I was idealistic and more than a little crazy. In my characteristic impulsive and narrowly focused way, I went full speed ahead. I committed to completing this project in one year, with 52 weeks on the calendar to keep me accountable. I had a dream and a deadline, and I did it—okay, I did need one extra week, but I explained why, and he was worth the wait. When I have a deadline, I can do it. There was no deadline to finish writing the book. I didn't do it in a timely manner.

I made myself accountable to myself (wow, that's scary) and set a deadline. It has drug on too long, and I promised 104 people I would get this done, and I will. There has to be a reason why it has taken me so long, and I know what it is. I just don't want to put it in print.

Perhaps, like many of my patients who skirt the word they are trying to use but can't produce by describing it—circumlocution, we call it in my trade—I will skirt the issue too. I will talk around it, I will describe it, but I won't actually *say* it.

I will tell you that I *wanted* to, I *tried* to make myself do it, but I simply didn't. Like any hard work that any normal human being avoids, I avoided writing this book. After a while, that brilliant and shiny idea lost its luster. Then it was simply an overlooked obligation. And, on the heels of my first two books that failed to earn a spot even in the bargain bin, I simply shut down. Why bother? I thought.

218

Because I committed to this, that's why I continue to bother. It is excruciating to sit myself down and force words onto my keyboard, but I told those 104 people I would, so here I am. Then there's Gina. Gina is looking down upon me and gently prodding me to keep my word to those 104 people, and to her, too. And, of course, my parents. They didn't let me off the hook from above, either. And they shouldn't have. Their lives and their deaths were the inspiration for this project.

No matter how long it takes me to deliver, I like to think I am a woman of my word. Just not in a timely manner. Obviously, since you are reading it, it is done. I am sorry and ashamed that I didn't do it more efficiently. I apologize for being a slacker, for—the word I was avoiding earlier---being *lazy*. I am human, and this humanness took over too many times. I neglected this living thing I conceived and gave birth to; I should probably be punished for that. Rest assured that I have berated myself many times, so with that, let's move on.

On to the reality that, while I had hoped it would bring about big changes in my patterns of interactions with some of these 52 people, I don't think I can call them big. I think perhaps there were some small, but significant changes in a few relationships, but for the rest, the memory of our lunch date will serve as a token of my love and affection for them. I hate to include this, but at least one of my lunch dates reported they reached out, and their lunch dates didn't reach back. They tried to form or fix a relationship, and it didn't happen. It ended with lunch. It was not all a success as was hoped.

Perhaps, however, it was not about me. Perhaps the ripple effect has reached far, farther than I could ever or will ever know. Perhaps there were connections made that changed lives in incredible ways that I will never know. I hope so.

I do know that several of my lunch dates made incredible changes in their lives as a direct result of *52 Lunch Dates*. Rhonda (August 17th) made peace with a high-school friend that she had been at odds with for over 30 years. They continue to see each other. Anita (March 23rd) made—and has kept—a commitment to herself to take time for her life, time to take others to lunch, or spending it in other ways. She also frequently takes lunch to a friend who is physically unable to leave her home. Ila (March 12th) reconnected with an old friend from high school who didn't know Ila was likely going to die. They got to see each other one more time before she died less than two months later.

I hope there are more far-reaching stories that I don't know about, but if not, this much is a bounty.

To all of you, *thank you*. I will treasure the memory of our lunch, and our friendship as well.

**

Life has a way of cycling. I am back to some old patterns that, for lack of a better explanation, seem to work for me. Most days, I am back to eating my lunch in the car, typically between my home health visits. With most of my friends, we are back in the same patterns of interaction. If I saw them once a month, I still see them once a month. If I saw them once a year, then once a year it is. If I hadn't seen them in years, well, you get the idea.

I had grand illusions of changing all this. I'm not sure what I expected, perhaps I thought we would all come to live in a sort of wonderland of friendship, whereby we would all just drop everything on a regular basis and go have lunch and hang out. We would shirk the responsibilities that could be shirked, some that shouldn't be, and simply *have more fun*. We would all come to see the importance of not only having fun, but of having friends, having health and happiness.

Short of that, my hope is that the lunch dates and the subsequent publishing of this book gave everyone in the book at least a small measure of each of those elements.

My appreciation of fun, friends, health, and happiness has multiplied, even if my actions don't show it. My life is rich and full, and my hope is that this book has shown that, and I wish the same for you.

Go ask someone you care about to lunch and ask them to *pay it forward*. And, if you so desire, feel free to write a book about it. You have my blessing.

ACKNOWLEDGMENTS

The most obvious thank-*yous* must first go to my 52-plus lunch dates, and your lunch dates. This project would not exist without you and your willingness to participate in this activity. Your patience with this crazy idea, and the prolonged time it took to finish it is appreciated more than you know.

My sons were much younger and still living at home for much of this epic project, and they granted me the time and quiet to work on it.

My husband has been with me throughout the project. He is a lunch date as well, (April 22nd), and a quiet but strong supporter of any idea—crazy or not—I decide to develop.

Tina (December 17th) was the catalyst for this project. It was her *"Let's do lunch"* comment that broke the camel's back—in a good way. I could no longer agree to it, or suggest it without doing it, as I had done many times before.

Rhonda (August 17th) kept me on my toes and working toward the completion of this book, because she wanted her incredible lunch date story in print, perhaps more than any other date. It truly embodies the spirit of this book. Her Pay-It-Forward date brought about incredible changes in her life, as well as her date's life.

Julie Hess, graphic artist extraordinaire and new friend (but too new to be a lunch date), deserves much thanks for conceiving and creating the cover of this book.

Laura Frances, author and Amazon publisher extraordinaire is to thank for helping me bring the whole project together, upload it and hit "publish" on Amazon. I call her a new friend, too.

To the handful of people who were lunch dates in the initial project, but were not included, either by their choice or by circumstance, you mean as much to me as all the others. To those who were not part of the first round, but agreed to round two, you are all first-rate.

Thank you everyone.

Made in the USA
Monee, IL
03 December 2023

48104669R00132